Architecture and the Public Good

Architecture and the Public Good

Tom Spector

ANTHEM PRESS

Anthem Press
An imprint of Wimbledon Publishing Company
www.anthempress.com

This edition first published in UK and USA 2025
by ANTHEM PRESS
75–76 Blackfriars Road, London SE1 8HA, UK
or PO Box 9779, London SW19 7ZG, UK
and
244 Madison Ave #116, New York, NY 10016, USA

First published in the UK and USA by Anthem Press in 2021

Copyright © Tom Spector 2025

The author asserts the moral right to be identified as the author of this work.

All rights reserved. Without limiting the rights under copyright reserved above,
no part of this publication may be reproduced, stored or introduced into
a retrieval system, or transmitted, in any form or by any means
(electronic, mechanical, photocopying, recording or otherwise),
without the prior written permission of both the copyright
owner and the above publisher of this book.

British Library Cataloguing-in-Publication Data
A catalogue record for this book is available from the British Library.

Library of Congress Control Number: 2024945220

ISBN-13: 978-1-83999-381-7 (Pbk)
ISBN-10: 1-83999-381-2 (Pbk)

Cover image: Image by Tom Spector.

This title is also available as an e-book.

CONTENTS

List of Figures vii
Acknowledgments ix

1. The Architecture Profession and the Public Good   1
2. The Architecture Profession in Capitalism   23
3. Who Is the Public?   55
4. Public and Private   83
5. Toward an Architecture of Publicness   107

Appendix 143
Notes 147
Bibliography 159
Index 167

FIGURES

1.1	Louis Kahn	2
1.2	Architecture culture map of the United States	8
2.1	2016 Revenues for the largest architecture firms	24
2.2	Rents increase as design quality increases in commercial office buildings	30
2.3	Chicago skyline	32
2.4	Boston Towers	33
2.5	Globalized AE revenues, 2016	43
3.1	Taksim Square, 2013	56
3.2	Tahrir Square, 2011	63
3.3	New York Firemen's Memorial, 1913. Harold Magonigle, architect	69
3.4	Vietnam Veterans' Memorial, 1982. Maya Lin, architect	72
3.5	Oklahoma City National Memorial and Museum, 2000. Butzer Design Partnership) (210 feet of the fence remain outside the memorial)	73
3.6	National 9/11 Memorial and Museum–2011. Michael Arad, architect; Peter Walker, landscape architect; and Daniel Libeskind, master plan	74
3.7	Empty Sky Memorial, New Jersey, 2011. Frederic Schwartz and Jessica Jamroz, Frederic Schwartz Architects	75
3.8	Trafalgar Square, Pride March, 2010	79
3.9	Black Lives Matter, Charlotte, NC	80
4.1	Isaiah Davenport House, Savannah, Georgia	84
4.2	San Francisco Lesbian-Gay-Bisexual-Transgender Community Center	92
4.3	Green-Meldrim House, Savannah	103
5.1	American Institute of Architects, September 12, 2017	108
5.2	The Capitol Mall, Washington, DC	114
5.3	The Archway at Rowes Wharf, Boston, SOM architects	116
5.4	Oklahoma City, Bricktown	119

5.5 San Francisco Federal Building, Morphosis and Smithgroup
architects 121
5.6 Salt Lake City Federal Courthouse, Thomas Phifer architects 122
5.7 San Francisco City Hall 125
5.8 California Academy of Sciences, San Francisco, Renzo Piano
Workshop, architects 126
5.9 City of Arts and Sciences, Valencia, Santiago
Calatrava, architect 127
5.10 British National Library, London, Colin St. John Wilson,
architect 128
5.11 *Biblioteque Nationale*, Paris, Dominique Perrault, architect 129
5.12 The Oculus, World Trade Center, New York, Santiago
Calatrava, architect 130

ACKNOWLEDGMENTS

The material and arguments in this book have been in development for a number of years. Parts of the argument have originally appeared in other publications and been tried out in other venues. A discussion of the coercive aspects of our codes of ethics was first aired at a conference convened at Cambridge University in 2003 by Nicholas Ray and Andrew Saint and later appeared as a chapter in the book *Architecture and Its Ethical Dilemmas* edited by Nick Ray. The problems with moral relativism under globalization were presented as a paper at the 2018 conference of the International Society for the Philosophy of Architecture in Colorado Springs.

A discussion of the disjunction between good design and good business was first tried out as a presentation at the London School of Economics in 2001 and presented in a revised form at the 2017 American Institute of Architects (AIA) North Dakota chapter conference. An essay on my interest in the applicability of Habermas's work on the public to thinking about architecture was presented at Newcastle University in 2010 and first appeared in print in the journal *Scroope* in 2011. A discussion of publics and counterpublics was presented in Boston in 2012. An essay on the need to acquaint feminist architecture and feminist ethics first appeared in the journal *Center* in 2007. I have tried out the concept of publicness on several occasions and in print as a chapter in the *Routledge Companion to Architecture and Social Engagement* edited by Farhan Karim. Many thanks to everyone who listened, read, questioned, and challenged me to improve.

Many thanks also to the peer reviewers at Anthem Press for their insights and criticism. You have improved this work. Finally, many thanks to Nick Ray, whose supportive criticism at various stages of this project were invaluable to its realization.

Chapter 1

THE ARCHITECTURE PROFESSION AND THE PUBLIC GOOD

Introduction

I love being an architect. My fellow architects' deep wells of idealism, artistry, and technical knowledge always challenge me to be better. But, as a profession, architecture needs improving. Our profession has struggled for so long to articulate a durable, convincing, and encompassing ethical place in the world that its vulnerability has become one of its regular features. Challenges to its legitimacy are both commonplace and come at us from several directions: indirectly from the forces of globalization which are transforming practice in ways that undermine moral agency, more pointedly from neoliberal economists who question the efficacy of all state protections and politicians who are suspicious of professional expertise, from related occupations seeking to improve themselves at our expense and, even from within, by an enduring fractiousness that leaves it relatively easy pickings for the others to invade or dismantle. Combine the unresolved tensions within the profession that have been with us from the outset with those external sources of attack, and you have a profession whose tenuous status is belied by the situation's ubiquity. If you've only ever lived in a tornado, then that is your normal. But we can step outside the swirl to envision a better way of practice so that the good of the profession prevails. To do this, however, we must understand and resolve our internal conflicts before we can turn our attention outward with both clarity and a common sense of purpose.

While a profession may well function as a locus for certain societal tensions—the legal profession prominently so—the architecture profession's internal conflict, created along the suture between art and service which in no small part defines it, unfortunately leads us to undermine our ethical mission in the world almost as soon as we assert it and, in the process, reduces the profession's potential as a force for good. This tendency toward self-abnegation asserted itself yet again in late 2020 when the American Institute of Architects' (AIA's) influential New York chapter, in response to the eruption of social justice protests of that summer, issued a high-minded statement against those

Figure 1.1 Louis Kahn
Source: Courtesy American Building Museum, Robert Lautman Collection

architects designing criminal justice facilities in the United States due to the deep-seated racism driving much of the criminal justice system, while only days later in London *The Guardian* reported on a spate of British architecture firms forcing their employees into fraudulently claiming pandemic furloughs.[1] Thus, while some architects push their national organization toward new ethical horizons, others are seeking to subvert the most basic moral responsibilities to their employees, to their fellow architects, and to a nation trying to ease the social cost of the pandemic crisis. This is how we undermine our best impulses and our determination to prove the profession's importance to the world. We look outward to champion the need to fight racism and global warming, to promote social justice in our cities, to encourage recycling, to achieve net zero emissions and cultural diversity in our work, while at the same time on the inside the profession makes little progress on its own racial diversity, drives women out of it, awards work glorifying autocrats, and fails to enforce the dignified treatment of its most vulnerable members. If we want to change our profession's standing in the world so that it can become a more effective force for its improvement, a strong place to start would be by doing a better job of living it.

The enduring fracture between art and service that lies at the root of this situation would not be so momentous were it the case that those practitioners whose actions do the most to undermine its ethical aspirations operated in the profession's dark and marginal crevices, like the medical profession's pill mills do. But the opposite is closer to the truth. Our famed artistic heroes are rarely our moral exemplars and our service champions go mostly unsung. We honor such important figures in modern architectural history as Louis Kahn, Frank Lloyd Wright, Mies van der Rohe, and Richard Meier whose art either requires disdain for such Enlightenment-based, middle-class niceties as prudence, temperance, justice, reduction of class differences, the nobility of all work and the ineliminable dignity of all persons—or else the ability to exercise such disdain is treated as a perk of their elite status.[2] The collective urge to shrug off architects' more embarrassing actions because art requires them cannot help but place stress on our claims to professionalism. The result is an ongoing, seemingly interminable, often impatient, and sometimes downright mean internal discourse over the art and service divide. How did things get this way?

Architecture's Culture of Patronage

Though the architecture profession as we know it, like most professions, owes its intellectual debt to the Enlightenment and its material origin to the Industrial Revolution, it has never fully rid itself of the culture of aristocratic patronage that sustained it prior to these transformative events. The distance between this eighteenth-century dedication to George III in a book by William Chambers:

> To THE KING. I HUMBLY beg leave to lay at Your Majesty's feet the following Dissertation upon an Art of which You are the first Judge, as well as the most munificent encourager [...] Your Majesty's dutiful servant and faithful subject, WILLIAM CHAMBERS.[3]

And Office of Metropolitan Architecture (OMA) partner Renier de Graaf's approving reference to a statement by Frank Gehry:

> I think the best thing is to have a benevolent dictator—who has taste![4]

is mainly one of formality, not intent, and it gestures to the idea that the remnants of the aristocratic patronage orientation have proven quite durable, though altered into what we know as the star system, into the present day in both education and in the maintenance of elite status. The architecture profession is particularly susceptible to a childlike desire for protective father figures, more so than other professions, because of its determination to favor the intangibles of art or design over such quantitative measures as profits, productivity increases, reductions in mortality or the number of people elevated out of poverty as primary indices of success. Achievement, then, is measured by how successfully the artist elevates his or her patrons above mere popularity.

Denise Scott Brown, who has been a close observer of this situation, understands well the implications of this determination: "Why do architects need to create stars? Because, I think, architecture deals with unmeasurables. Although architecture is both science and art, architects stand or fall in their own estimation and in that of their peers by whether they are 'good designers,' and the criteria for this are ill-defined and undefinable."[5] Scott Brown suggests that, lacking objective criteria, a persona ("a guru") must stand in as the object of desire or criticism. That persona's ability to answer to no one and run roughshod over others becomes a success indicator. Thomas Fisher writes that this orientation hurts the profession's ability to assert its societal benefits: "Our design culture, ironically, may present the greatest hurdle to demonstrating our value."[6] Indeed, as we shall see, many of the claims architects make lack hard evidence. Fisher points out that architects surely have a significant role in quantifiable public welfare functions, such as enhanced energy savings, but is quick to say that architects do a poor job of quantifying the results:

> Too many in the profession hold on to the out-of-date idea that quantifying the effects of design somehow diminishes it and destroys its mystique, an idea that mystifies most people outside of the profession and that lessens our influence. Add to that the equally antiquated idea of the "gentleman" architect who shouldn't appear to need or want money—a self-fulfilling prophecy that too many clients have been all too happy to oblige.[7]

The profession's vacillation between art and service—haughty artists held up as mirrors of real achievement, but emphasizing service when presenting itself to outsiders—greatly explains why it has never resolved these tensions in the training of future architects. The tensions originated in the nineteenth century, where the pinnacle of architectural training, the *Ecole des Beaux-Arts*, was entirely patronage oriented. Prospective students—*nouveaus*—seeking entry at the *Ecole* could apply directly by way of portfolio or instead sign up to learn directly under the tutelage of an established master who was not part of the *Ecole*. Students, not enrolled in the *Ecole*, trained in these ateliers with the hopes of passing the entrance exam and those who were already in the *Ecole* sought recognition through their association with a known practicing master. The masters ran their ateliers as status symbols of their greatness. Their students' success at the *Ecole* and at the annual Salon not only reaffirmed their masters' greatness but also brought more commissions. Success bred success. The greater the master, the more talented students wanted to associate and align themselves with a proven track record at both the *Ecole* and the Salon.

Competition among the independent ateliers meant that the *Ecole* could raise the bar even higher guarantying that it would get only the best of the best.

Neither the *Ecole* nor the ateliers taught in any organized way the mechanics of putting buildings together. According to Jean-Paul Carlhian,

> It never attempted to nor ever had the pretention of teaching architecture: it was not a professional school by any stretch of the imagination. What institution whose curriculum never required more than two exercises requiring the drawing of wall sections would ever aspire to such a reputation? The *Ecole*, in the mold of many a French institution of higher learning, concerned itself with the shaping and training of minds: it aspired to teach future architects how to think, architecturally; and by introducing them to a carefully devised multiplicity of exercises exposed them, time and again, to the exercise of judgement.[8]

A contemporary account by John Meade Howells of the *Ecole* system may sound disturbingly real to employees of some firms today. The *nouveaus* were treated abominably: "The atelier is, in its way, like a tiny republic—a slaveholding one, I was going to say, for the *nouveau* is an actual slave, though without the hopelessness of real slavery, since he is at the same time the embryonic *ancien*."[9] As with the modern elite office, without the *nouveau*, "the atelier could not exist; and this is primarily a matter of ways and means."[10] "In the atelier world, then, simply two classes exist: the *ancien*, who is everything; the *nouveau*, who is nothing. A third and higher class might be added, a sort of high-priesthood, surrounded in its isolation by a strict doctrine of infallibility."[11]

After the *Ecole* was dethroned as the standard-bearer of architectural education by modernism, the Bauhaus sought to provide an example for the democratization of the culture of patronage:

> Gropius eliminated such traditional, hierarchical, and status-oriented titles as professor and student, substituting instead the term master and, for the varying levels of students, apprentices, journeymen (those how had passed the first examination set by the Weimar's local guilds), and junior masters [...] Yet despite the Manifesto's elevated claims and the new titles for students and professors, the Bauhaus was little more than a conventional academy when it opened its doors to its initial 150 students.[12]

Apparently, these attempts at democratization were more thorough with the art and design students than with the architects, whose work had some market value. By 1922, "Whispered complaints about Gropius's use of publicly subsidized Bauhaus students in his private architectural office began to be heard."[13] Thus, the conditions of slave labor of future architects crept in anyway.

Even though the *Ecole des Beaux-Arts* artistic values became superseded by those of modernism, the school's aristocratic attitude toward work, in which a student's investment of time is treated as infinite and therefore valueless, combined with the patronage orientation in which the master holds the keys to the mysteries of design, has remained part of the culture in both modern schools and elite offices. This is precisely how Louis Kahn's office operated. In Kahn's office, young employees

> rarely stayed for more than a year or two; they returned home or simply had to make more money because we often didn't get paid for four or five weeks at a time [...] it's also something that you can't really emulate. I tried that in the early days of my own office, but it really didn't work. You have to pay the bills. So, the world is certainly blessed with Kahn's work, but it's a very rare thing.[14]

About the persistence of this orientation, Denise Scott-Brown has observed: "The authoritarian personalities and the we-happy-few culture engendered by the *Beaux-Arts* stayed on in Modern architecture long after the *Beaux-Arts* architectural philosophy had been abandoned."[15] The direct repercussions of this orientation can be found in the difficulty the profession has in establishing its value to the outside world, in the frequency with which its practitioners ignore the basics of fair labor practices, and in its reluctance to call out sexual harassment of employees at all levels.

As any fraternity brother knows, hazing builds both camaraderie and resilience while it inculcates the status quo. Howells describes a demeaning event which consisted of meanly clad *nouveaux* being paraded down a Parisian street to the sound of brass instruments, while being sprayed with cold water. While this hazing ceremony might have been unpleasant, at least it had the virtue of being overtly what it was.[16] Too much hazing goes on today under the guise of other names. As Stella Lee says,

> To really effect change, we need to focus on culture, and where it is solidified—in education. Architectural education is plagued by the mentality that suffering is a necessary part of its practice. Sleepless nights and poor self-care seem to be par for the course for creative production. As a guest juror at a university architecture department, I once watched in horror as a student fainted from lack of sleep during her presentation.[17]

Nowadays, employers are more sophisticated. They treat employees as either friends, management, or fellow team members, and thereby insinuate that everyone is responsible for pulling his or her share of the load—but the trick is that only the employer or manager gets to define the load. These are exactly the sorts of tactics used by the British firms against their employees during the Covid-19 pandemic which were exposed in *The Guardian*. This modern hazing leads to a version of Stockholm syndrome among employees who become the enforcers when a young employee stubbornly insists that he or she will only work a standard week. According to Andrew Maynard,

> This attitude, as expected, put me on a crash course with management. When it was clear that I was going to be uncompromising my employer became passive aggressive and easily rallied a handful of fellow employees against me. I was accused of not being a team player. I was accused of not being committed to my projects. The quiet hostility got to the point where I found it necessary to have my employment agreement front-and-centre on my desk, conveniently flipped to the page stating that my work day ceased at 5.30 pm and my right to paid overtime should I work beyond this.[18]

The number one factor in achieving the star status Scott Brown discusses earlier is having worked for a star architect. Thus, patronage for those seeking elite status is crucial. Indeed, the importance of this patronage from the star is so pronounced that, according to Roxanne Williamson, who has studied the phenomenon, "the important constant in the professional lives of famous architects is the apprenticeship connection; other factors, although important, are secondary [...] My conclusion, however, is not that genius seeks genius, but that under certain circumstances genius creates genius."[19] Williamson compiled a list of 247 famous architects, starting with Thomas Jefferson and finishing in 1982 from mentions in 24 books about architecture. She found that the timing of the contact between young, future famous architects and their famous employers was significant. If the young architect was working for the famous architect when the famous architect was experiencing his or her breakout period, then this coincidence greatly improved the young architect's chances for fame. Once the fame of the older architect is well established, employment within that firm as a predictor of future fame declines. Of that 247, only 38 were what Williamson termed "loners" who had no direct link to a famous employer, colleague or employee early in their careers.

The patronage connection grinds to a halt the democratization of cultural influence and with it, an important component of professional meritocracy. Even as the American population spread southward in recent decades there has been no corresponding dispersal of reputation-building magazine coverage. A map of architects' cultural influence in the United States based on publication frequency in *Architectural Record* shows a top-heavy preference for New York City architects who received one-third of all coverage while constituting only 3 percent of the nation's architects. California holds its own, but such important electoral states as Texas and Florida shrivel into insignificance while a number of states disappear from the map altogether (see Appendix A).

Williamson concludes with some concerns regarding the coercive aspects of architectural fame: "Is the system that created our boldest architects fixed? Are the mechanics of fame so rigid that they will continue to preselect nearly all of those architects who will be the leaders of the profession? Does it exclude many with potential?"[20] While accepting Williamson's and *Favored Circle* author Garry Stevens's similar diagnosis of the mechanics of fame in architecture, we need not share their concern for how we might democratize access to fame (Williamson), or how to accept the status quo (Stevens), and instead determine to turn our backs on the fame game altogether because it perverts how a profession should work.

The mystique of the great creator, the need for patronage, and aristocratic disdain for the measurable combine to lead ever so naturally to an underground culture of harassment in the workplace. As Stella Lee says:

> The acceptance of suffering easily slips into normalizing sexual misconduct and its suppression as simply part of the practice. Cultlike worship of the star architect only exacerbates this condition, and there are plenty

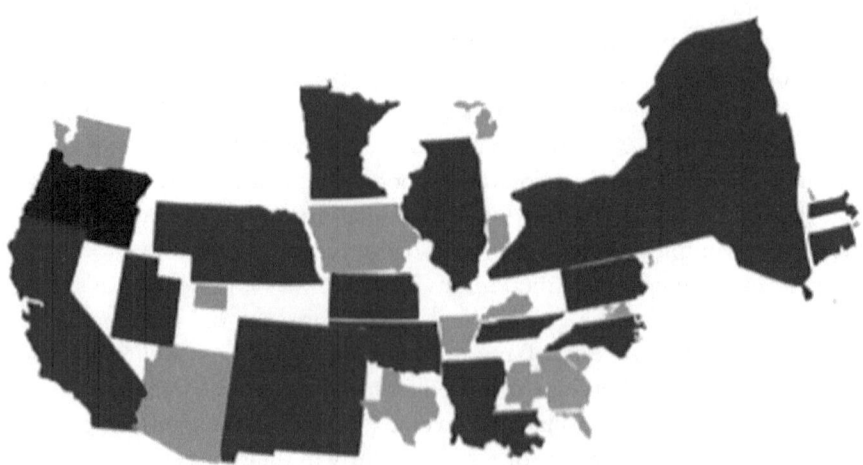

Figure 1.2 Architecture culture map of the United States
Source: Tom Spector

of those who work for these so-called star architects, willing to sacrifice their time and integrity because they have been conditioned to believe that this mode of production is normal.[21]

When the RIBA wondered why fully half the women that go into the architecture profession in Britain leave it, the report it commissioned concluded that it was precisely the culture that was the heart of the problem—the decision to leave was due to a constant clash of values. It would seem, the profession can scarcely afford the drain of half of its architecture-school trained women bailing on it, yet the phenomenon is widespread. A similar study in Australia had similar findings.[22]

In a well-publicized 1996 effort to transform schools of architecture away from this thinking, the influential Carnegie Foundation report on architectural education recommended that schools of architecture:

- Establish a climate of engagement
- Clarify the public benefits of architecture
- Promote the creation of new knowledge
- Stress the critical importance of ethical professional behavior.[23]

The authors, Ernest L. Boyer and Lee D. Mitgang, thought that these goals could be advanced by promoting civic activism and community service projects, but this cannot be a full answer if the profession has yet to successfully articulate the good it does; unless it intends to make community service projects a part of architects' everyday activities.

To make a more substantive ethical commitment in their practices, some firms do supplement their for-profit activities with pro bono work. Approximately half of all firms report engaging in some sort of pro bono work (there are no standards, however, for determining what counts as pro bono). Pro bono defending of the indigent is fundamental to the ethical remit of the legal profession, but we should beware of trying to legitimate the activities of an entire occupation on what amounts to a bit of crust accomplished when things get slow at the office or by providing financial support for those who do good works full time. There are no moral proxies. It is unlikely that pro bono work and civic activism get to the heart of the matter any more so than the Southern Poverty Law Center and Doctors Without Borders provide ethical justification for the legal and medical professions, however laudable their efforts to represent the impoverished or treat people unfortunate enough to live in war zones. What such efforts do achieve is twofold: they show a different side of professions from the everyday work they engage in and they do a certain socially beneficial service in the process. But these side engagements in themselves would not be enough to necessitate a state-protected profession's existence. The core societal good must accrue directly from the myriad everyday transactions between professionals and their clients if it is to be something we claim as both normative and action-guiding.

The Carnegie report's authors think that the clarification task involves more effective communication skills—always desirable, but still—to be able to "advocate with clarity for the beauty, utility, and ecological soundness of the built environment."[24] But the fundamental stumbling block here is not the advocacy, it's the clarity. The report assumes that these benefits are well defined, just not well publicized. We can see how these calls to elucidate them then easily lapse into publicity campaigns. "Educators and the profession simply must make better known what architecture can contribute to fulfilling human needs and promoting more wholesome communities."[25] Later they describe the purpose of architectural education and of architectural practice as "making life more comfortable, pleasurable, secure, and productive for all citizens, including the disenfranchised in our society."[26] and they want to cultivate the "capacity of architectural design to enrich community life ."[27] All worthy things, but they lead us away from the issues in education that are most to blame for the culture of patronage that lies at the origin of the profession's inner tensions.

Ending the attitude of overlooking labor exploitation that begins in school is a necessary first step toward creating an ethical architectural culture that can be a force for improving the world. According to even a cursory reading of the Fair Labor Standards Act in the United States, young architectural employees will rarely meet the criteria necessary to be legally considered eligible for the management, independent subcontractor, or of creative professional employee exemptions from overtime pay.[28] Refusing to aggressively police the profession on this issue not only props up the fame machine for the few, but it does so on the backs of the rank and file who are actually helping secure the long-term legitimacy of the profession by placing these practitioners at a competitive disadvantage. Architects who pay little to nothing for their labor are simply better placed to create aesthetically adventurous work for the same money. The AIA has never published guidance on this important matter, as a first step toward reducing its prevalence, even though it has its own attorneys fully capable of evaluating the applicable laws. Our professional organizations, accreditation boards, and governing bodies could do much more than they do to enforce a culture that no longer depends on labor exploitation They can publicize the ethical treatment of labor, create supportive venues for reporting transgressions, and take active steps to punish transgressors. If the profession routinely fails to protect the most vulnerable within its own confines, then how can it be expected to act with greater care towards those outside?

Our Ambivalent Defense of the Profession

Recognizing that art is a fraught basis for asserting state protection of both its practices and title, our professional organizations and our governing boards try to gloss over the internal conflict by hinging the profession's legitimacy on its unique role in promoting the public health, safety, and welfare, or more succinctly, the public good that results from such protection, even though clearly stating just what that good consists of eludes them as much as it eludes the authors of the Carnegie report. To illustrate the convulsions the profession puts itself through when trying to defend its public welfare function consider this news item and institutional response released by the AIA in 2018, which introduces both an external source of attack and a response weakened by ambivalence:

> Approximately 25 states are in the process of shrinking licensure requirements through legislation or executive actions.

Now, while not all these efforts are narrowly targeting architects, the AIA fears that such efforts can *potentially endanger the health, safety, and welfare of the public.*

(Let us hasten to add that this is not an exclusively American phenomenon. The United Kingdom has seen its share of attempts at de-professionalization since the 1980s as have other countries.) The AIA's response is to construct a loose syllogism:

> Simply stated, our message is:

- Architects study and train extensively and become licensed to help ensure the health, safety and welfare of all who occupy and visit the structures that they design.
- All U.S. states and territories require a license to practice architecture as a means to ensure buildings are safe for their occupants and the public.
- The AIA believes the public is best served when state regulatory boards, duly constituted under state law, are free to regulate professional licensure on behalf of the public and consumers.[29]

Note how many times "the public" is invoked in this statement. But where in it is the standard of service mentioned (or even implied), except for safety, to which architects should hold themselves and against which the profession should be policed? The mere fact that state-sanctioned licensure is commonplace in the United States does not constitute an argument that such protections are desirable. It is only a data point. What is the basis for this belief in state-sanctioned licensure as the surest route to public service? What facts and logic can we bring to support it? How do we even know when a fully ethical justification has been offered? At minimum, it is reasonable to ask such a justification to address the following:

- The justification has to engage in matters of importance. Failing this, ethics fails to enter the picture.
- The justification has to be central to what architects spend a significant amount of their time actually doing. Justifying an activity based on its marginal actions or indirect benefits gives too little on which to build a strong justification.
- Such a justification must be based in the reality that the profession exists as a creature of the capitalist economic system, yet its benefits cannot be totally consumed by profit motives if professionalism isn't to be crowded out of the equation. If the benefits of architecture are completely consumed by the profit motive, then the self-policing aspects of capitalism—the ability to raise capital, bankruptcy, absorption—should be adequate to determine who should and who should not be in business, just as in, say, the restaurant business.
- It must also somehow go beyond the merely legal if the ethical isn't to be reduced to the purely prudent observing of regulations.

I propose that architecture practiced as a state-protected profession or under a protected title does indeed serve an important benefit to the public health, safety, and welfare that could not be well served purely by market mechanisms in a deregulated industry but that we have labored under a fuzzy idea of just how that happens. We invoke the public good but have neglected to define it. We have neglected the public in no small part because the patronage orientation pushes it to the margins but there are other reasons as well.

The public has also been neglected in recent years especially due to the exacerbating effects globalized capital has placed on practice. Although economic globalization has been a force for lifting billions of people out of abject poverty, globalization has brought with it several unwanted actions in its wake. It makes the public ever more distant, ever more abstract, when projects are far-flung across the globe. It compresses the workforce, even the architecture workforce it touches, into a relatively few upper managers and stockholders on the one hand, and labor on the other. This compression makes individual agency all the more difficult to exercise and to track the effects of one's actions: Moral action requires moral agents. Economic globalization has also played a crucial role in accelerating climate change but without helping to create correspondingly global incentives, or even concepts, for reversing carbon-forcing—making it all the more difficult for well-meaning architects to play a substantial role in either reversing the course or helping people make adjustments to its looming effects.

We have neglected it because we think we already know what we mean by the public, but we do not. We think that, by the word "public," we mean something like "everyone" or possibly, the government, but it is far from clear that "everyone" is of like mind in what they want, or if they are, it is only at a very low common denominator and it is even more doubtful that the government is an adequate proxy for what the public should want. Just as likely, the government is part of the problem or most commonly, simply inadequate to the task of providing such a good in pluralist societies. We think of the public as a constant, of having always existed, and this is not true either. It has both a history emanating out of the Enlightenment and a trajectory into the present day.

We think of the public as transcending politics. But neither is this the case. The Enlightenment concept of the public of which we are the inheritors was initially and continues to be polemical. It reflects and promotes a definable set of values as a realm that speaks to power but is not itself state power. This feature makes our modern conception distinctly different from the ancient Greek *polis* which was itself an exercise in state power.

Finally, we think of the public and its complement, the private realm, as capable of being clearly demarcated from each other. This is yet another misleading assumption. The question of what is legitimately public and what private is both shifting and contentious. If we can be this mistaken about the public—who is in it, where it came from, what it stands for, and what lies outside it—then it only makes sense we would have trouble defining our ethical role as architects in it.

This leaves the subject of public welfare as a directly pursued component of architecture, unsurprisingly, poorly executed. It is more likely that this somewhat vague concept of public welfare is supposed to emerge holistically as a supervening quality more than it is a concept with specific criteria for success. But how are we supposed to put our arms around something that evanescent?

If the public health, safety, and welfare are the terms with which we justify ourselves as a profession, then the criteria for justification require that they should also be terms central to what we teach and how we practice. It won't do that these goods are indirectly produced by professionalized architects because that outcome only begs the question of what would be a more direct way of producing such goods. Like justifying the NASA space program because it resulted in some new products for the home, we wonder why not just develop those products without the costly middleman? But in actual practice, client service and personal achievement occupy the center with public safety narrowly construed as constraints to the pursuit of the first two. The public welfare function architecture serves then, is fulfilled by observing the building codes and land use regulations that limit the space of possible action. These constraints are inadequate, however, to function as goals—the goal to meet the building code doesn't aim very high, nor is it broad enough to inform most of our work activity. It does describe something worthwhile but it's not enough.

Prizing artistry as a public good creates a fraught bargain because artistry, for all its possible ameliorating effects on otherwise impoverished built environments, is just as readily used to distance its creators and commissioners from public acceptance. The attitude is so ingrained that modest proposals to rethink it can be greeted with shrill responses. When Steven Bingler and Martin C. Peterson opined in the *New York Times* that,

> For too long, our profession has flatly dismissed the general public's take on our work, even as we talk about making that work more relevant with worthy ideas like sustainability, smart growth and "resilience planning" […] The problem isn't the infinitesimal speck of buildings created by celebrity architects (some arresting, some almost comic in their dysfunction), but rather the distorting influence these projects have had on the values and ambitions of the profession's middle ranks[…] rediscovering the radical middle, where we meet, listen and truly collaborate with the public, speak a common language and still advance the art of architecture—is long overdue.[30]

they were heckled in the pages of *Architect* by Aaron Betsky: "The fact that buildings look strange to some people, and that roofs sometimes leak, is part and parcel of the research and development aspect of the design discipline."[31] Betsky, however, is partially right when he asserts that, "The truth is that architecture is not made by or for 'a wide spectrum of the population.' It is made for those who have the means to commission it, and reflects their values and priorities."[32] But if this were all there was to it, then there would be no justification for treating it as a profession. And perhaps that is something he doesn't care about. He sees a stark choice: "Architecture, in other words, is either the dull affirmation of what we have, or it is an attempt to make our world better."[33] This seems a false dichotomy but not a lacuna we need to take up here because not much hinges on its truth or falsity. The point is that it appears that the only route Betsky sees to making the world better is through elitist means and an aristocratic patronage orientation. What if disarming aristocracy *is* a path to making the world better? This possibility doesn't seem to occur to him or if it does, is not to be taken seriously. The AIA, as befits its attempts to please everyone all the time, wants both: it wants to assert a public orientation, at the same time it wants to provide cover for the elites. The result is, as ever, a weak and vacillating response. Betsky sees the orientation toward the public as consisting in "mystical appeals." And perhaps they have been mystical since the public has been a chimera. This sort of response fits perfectly with the strategies necessary to keep architecture within the field of restricted cultural consumption discussed by French sociologist Pierre Bourdieu: "Modernist architecture, like Modern art, has tended to be a revolt against bourgeois taste (and values): If granny, abuelita, or bubbe is for it, they're against it."[34]

Now, to some degree, this divergence of values between a profession and the those it serves is inevitable. Physicians certainly want people to value living healthy lifestyles free from cigarettes, with plenty of exercise, and going easy on deep-fried foods more than they evidently do value them. And architects can be forgiven for placing greater emphasis on the importance of artistic merit in buildings than do a lot of other people. However, we must constantly work to reduce that divergence to avoid the undesirable poles of debilitating conflict between professional insiders and public outsiders on the one hand, and outright irrelevance on the other. But even so, while it is a rare person indeed who doesn't understand the value of good health—even if they dislike pursuing it—it is not uncommon to find people unpersuaded by either the inherent value of contemporary architecture or the protected status of those who practice it. A logical starting point for explaining this divergence of values as deriving from a heightened sense of responsibility rather than heedlessness would be in a profession's code of ethics.

Ambivalence Reaches into Our Codes of Ethics

It has been observed that the problem with introducing a sense of class consciousness into the United States is that its motto of being a land of opportunity has led most Americans to consider themselves as either rich or pre-rich. We can point to a similar attitude operating in the society of architects, except that it operates with a different form of currency. That is, architects are led to consider themselves either as famous or pre-famous. In both cases, the masses are encouraged to self-identify with the elites, regardless of whether any realistic possibility of achieving that exalted status exists or not. I intend to argue that this attitude helps explain much of what comes to be expressed (as well as omitted) in architects' codes of ethics and professional conduct on both sides of the Atlantic, and that in reciprocal fashion, our codes of ethics and professional conduct do more to help sustain the practices of the elites in our profession than they do to actually express what we might think of as our ideals or our cherished values. That is, to be blunt about it, our published codes of ethics are as likely to be ideological weapons used by one class of members of the profession to coerce the rest, as they are to reflect the values architects actually live by as they trudge on against the forces of indifference, ugliness, unnecessary waste, shoddiness, environmental degradation, racism and all the rest in their practices and daily lives.

The ARB and the RIBA Standards

While the United States has its AIA Code of Ethics and registration laws that vary a bit from state to state, the United Kingdom has two main sources for standards of ethical professional behavior—the ARB Standards of Conduct and Practice, and the RIBA Code of Professional Conduct. The ARB Architects Code details standards to follow to meet the following expectations:

> Honesty, integrity, competence, responsible self-promotion, consider the wider impacts, conscientiousness, trustworthiness, carrying proper insurance, care of reputation, resolve complaints, cooperate with regulators, respect for others.

It should be noted that these standards are aimed primarily at clarifying the architect's responsibilities toward the client. Fair enough. The standard concerned with considering the wider impacts is brief: "Where appropriate, you should advise your client how best to conserve and enhance the quality of the environment and its natural resources."[35]

That's it. That's the entire scope of the architects' standards of practice. If the public good is important to British architects, it may be too vague to be placed in their standards. This lack has not gone unremarked. Simon Foxell has observed that,

> In an era that stresses service delivery over public obligation it is unclear how the institutions currently understand their public service remit and in what way it influences their activities. All of them have, to an extent, a public facing role, although this can vary considerably. They organize lectures, hold exhibitions, run award schemes, work with politicians to promote their part of the industry and run workshops with schoolchildren to encourage them into the profession. They have a direct interest in maintaining and improving the standards in their discipline and ensuring the skill levels of their members are adequate to be able to deliver them. What they don't have is a clearly articulated narrative explaining their public interest obligations either to themselves, the public or even to the Privy Council, the body responsible for their charters.[36]

Now, it could fairly be argued that the purpose of the ARB is not, nor should it be, to articulate ideals and values. It is doing what it is designed to do: to prescribe to architects and the public certain minimum standards of decency that, if not met, could result in some form of punishment.[37] But the justification of having standards at all is that they spell out requirements that somehow differ from ordinary expectations. To differ, then, these standards of decency must either be more stringent or else have additional content to them than would ordinary business practice. In other words, there would be no requirement for, say, travel agents to be as honest or as careful with client's money as architects, or else if these standards are the same, there must be some additional ones in the list that apply to the peculiar conditions of being an architect instead of being a travel agent. The first is probably not true: I would expect my travel agent to tell me, for example, which cruise ships had recently had outbreaks of food poisoning regardless of how much money the cruise line dangled in his face to book cruises, or to tell me if he had a financial interest in the vacation cabin he wants to rent to me. The standards of decency are probably about as high in both cases. But the second almost certainly is true: additional standards exist which apply uniquely to the practice of architecture. I wouldn't necessarily expect the travel agent to carry professional liability insurance, for example. This being granted, except for the aforementioned standard to consider the wider impacts of one's work, there is unfortunately precious little of that sort of distinctive content in the ARB standards. So little in fact that it calls into question the efficacy of having a distinctive set of standards that applies to architects that shouldn't be equally actionable against any other businessperson. As Jeremy Till observes, they are standards that "even my hairdresser could meet."[38] If my grocer sells me red cabbage and charges me for radicchio, I believe I have recourse, regardless of whether he has violated the grocer's code of conduct or not or even whether there is a grocer's code of conduct. In other words, just by virtue of living in civil society, certain minimal expectations adhere.

Unfortunately, what the ARB provides is minimal as well and the RIBA's foundational concerns for honesty, integrity, and competence, "as well as concern for others and for the environment"[39] provide little of substantial difference (although the admonition in Section 3.5 against modern slavery does jump out a bit from the fray as something we can all unreservedly support).

"Well," we might be tempted to say, "This is just the way codes of conduct are. They are bound to fail to capture our most deeply felt motives, the things we feel most passionate about." A reasonable response, but a look at other professions' codes of conduct reveals it to be misguided. Both the American Medical Association and the National Society of Professional Engineers, to take but two examples, have codes of ethics that are substantive, activist, and action-guiding. This in not just the way codes inevitably are. It is just the way ours is. *The Edge Commission Report on the Future of Professionalism* asserts much the same thing while finding the expression of a public-spirited ethic eminently achievable. According to Paul Morrell,

> It would therefore be genuinely in the public interest if the institutions were to clarify and codify exactly how they understand the term 'the public interest' in pursuit of the obligations of their charters, and produce (as for ethics) a rigorous, harmonised view of their expectations, both on behalf of themselves and of their members. This would include articulating the issues that arise, engaging with the public, raising the profile of public interest with members (as for ethical issues) and giving them the practical guidance – specifically as to the extent to which their conduct and practice should be modified to acknowledge a duty that extends beyond the immediate one owed to clients.[40]

When the ethic of practice expresses precious little more than that demanded of any business, the profession is vulnerable to denial of its ethical premises. This vulnerability ought to be perplexing, for if public opinion in the United Kingdom at all resembles that in the United States, architects are admired and hold a durable and substantial level of approval. Outsider sentiment appears comfortable with the idea of having someone held centrally responsible for whatever it is that the popular opinion of the architect's role consists of. Is the ethical basis for architectural practice, the sense that architects are engaged in a valued contract with the public for its protection in a way that cannot be equally well served by other arrangements, likely to arise out of the pages of *Architectural Record* and the other glossies, or is it more likely to generate itself out of the much more ubiquitous actions of the rank and file? This question is perhaps easier to answer if we consider the likely basis for approval of other professions: Is the widespread approval of the medical profession more likely to emanate from the millions of everyday transactions between physicians and their patients, or from the headline-grabbing news items about artificial hearts, in vitro fertilization, and other research advances?

Furthermore, this lack of content is made doubly unfortunate, if you believe (as I do) that the majority of fellow practitioners are, in fact, highly motivated to do the right thing, eager to make the world a better place, keen to create the best buildings they can according to the widest possible definition of the good. They hold themselves to higher—much higher—standards of behavior than the ARB, RIBA, and it should be added at this point, the AIA codes of conduct would suggest. (Fully two-thirds of the AIA code of ethics and professional conduct is devoted to instructing its members to obey various laws or to tell the truth!) So why isn't the practice of architecture described in motivational and discipline-specific terms? This is the question the discussion thus far has been preparing to take up. Why is the architecture profession so willing to leave itself vulnerable to critics of its unwillingness to hold itself to a high standard of public protection and service? It all comes back to its aristocratic orientation.

Codes and Coercion

What the AIA Code of Ethics, the ARB Code of Conduct, and the RIBA Principles do achieve is to avoid holding the profession's elite practitioners to standards they might find objectionable in their role as the guardians of disciplinary autonomy, while at the same time providing barely enough cover in the way of standards of behavior so that the discipline can enjoy the fruits of being a profession, with its restrictive barriers to entry, state protection of its practices, and promise of prosecution to those who claim the status without having gone through the hoops. Keeping a veneer of public service through professional codes of conduct helps the entire profession maintain its status, but keeping that veneer as thin and flexible as possible primarily benefits the guardians of the profession's autonomy by placing the lightest restrictions on their prerogatives. Thus, *of course* the current standards of conduct fail to overtly express most architects' basic values. They are systematically designed to avoid mentioning them.

Until 1979, statements of the AIA's highest expression of its values included the unethical behavior of both advertising and of competing with one another on the basis of fees. These elitist provisions were not rejected by the AIA leadership as unfairly favoring established practices; they were only cast out under the threat of antitrust action by the US Justice Department during its better days. Indeed, if enforcement and implementation of the RIBA's code of conduct resembles that of the AIA's, it will be the case that fully 70 percent of all enforcement actions respond to complaints by architects against other architects. The AIA's ethics board is preoccupied with policing the buddy system of giving each other proper credit for contributions toward a project. Clients and the public simply do not perceive the code of ethics as a viable vehicle for having grievances addressed. Out of America's 80,000 registered architects, who belonged to the AIA (the organization had over 95,000 members in 2020), over a 10-year period, only 13 ethics prosecutions were brought to the board by a either a client or a member of the public. This, despite the fact that fully two-thirds of the code is devoted to discussing the architect's relationship to the client and the public, and only one-fourth to how architects are to respect one another.

The lack of a substantive ethic of practice grounded in a strong commitment to public service is entirely consistent with a reluctance to limit disciplinary autonomy to pursue and create the most aesthetically daring work. A substantive ethic of practice grounded in public service must be portrayed as a form of weakness, or perhaps, an excuse for limited talent. And so it is, IF the real task is to further the discipline's autonomy.

Someone in a small town or regional practice who takes the idea of practicing architecture as a necessary community service places himself or herself at a double or triple disadvantage for rewards within the profession. Not only does such a practitioner suffer diminished opportunities for securing attention-getting work, but by committing to serving the community as it wishes to be served, such a practitioner is not engaging in the "critical" autonomy-increasing practices the profession most rewards. But what doubles down on all this, in addition to the vastly reduced opportunity and the self-blaming implication that a lack of talent is the culprit is that it is actually this sort of practitioner's actions that are most likely to give the profession its most enduring source of public respectability and hence make it all the easier for the elites to maintain their autonomy (by allowing the actions of ordinary practitioners to help serve as a filter and gatekeeper, as well as a referendum on the practices of the elite). The elites induce the rank and file to do this necessary job of securing a measure of public assent, which tends to keep the rank and file in its place

at the same time it blames the rank and filer for his own inferior status, and this makes the whole project, including the deliberately weak code of ethics, coercive. The idea of the meritocracy holds true, but in its current incarnation it is perverse because it actually tends to reward an outlook that diminishes an ethical regard for one's professional obligations. At the same time, it flourishes most (by providing the greatest opportunities for being built) if someone else is doing the necessary ethical work of earning public approval and confidence.

Some Partial Prescriptions for Change

A code of ethics worthy of its name cannot be prescribed by one angry author: it can only emerge out of intense and widespread debate. But, if this chapter is to conclude by speculating briefly on what a noncoercive code of ethics—one that helps us resist undermining our best impulses—might look like, what might emerge?

First, and obviously, architects might propose an unequivocal recognition of the crucial importance of actually behaving both responsibly and helpfully toward those in the profession who are most vulnerable: the interns and recent graduates trying to get on their feet in the working world while striving for competence and respect, as well as underrepresented groups and those most likely to suffer in hostile work environments. While recent iterations of the AIA, ARB, and RIBA codes have moved in this direction, there is much to be done to flesh out what these expectations should mean in daily practice. Those professionals who finance their "critical" practices on the backs of their young workers by circumventing employment laws, or who take no interest in their professional development, should not be praised. They should be prosecuted.

Second, the profession may want to formally recognize that it derives its legitimacy from public approval, and that this approval derives in turn from public perception that the actions of architects provide important protections for its health, safety, and welfare. The public is unlikely to license someone simply for his or her art. Architects who are unwilling to subscribe to this sort of ethic of public responsiveness because it would infringe upon their art are putting the legitimacy of the entire profession at risk.

Coupled with these ideas might be a statement of what architects consider to be motivating, unless we are somewhat ashamed of our motives. The existing codes of conduct certainly raises this possibility. Does anyone go through the exhaustion of architecture school, the humiliation of seeing professionals of other stripes who are similarly educated earn vastly greater sums, and suffer the public scrutiny of their work; does anyone go through all this for the sake of a single line in the AIA, ARB, or RIBA Codes of Ethics? After the egotistical thrills of influencing the expenditure of vast sums of money and of getting to see one's idea actually built begin to mellow, most of us suffer all this for the sake of a dream to make the world a more beautiful and humane place, if only a little, through our efforts. And, we hope, for the pleasure of being occasionally recognized and appreciated for having done so. This dream is what ultimately makes it all tolerable.

Finally, the profession could vastly improve its document by striking out of its current code of conduct provisions that apply to any businessperson operating any business. If this leaves the codes of conduct less than half a page long, so much the better. To be so lengthy, the current code's sins are almost entirely those of omission. To articulate a code of conduct of public service, both a consensus and much clarification is needed. Subsequent chapters of this book attempt to provide at least the beginnings of that clarification and the basis for consensus building.

The picture I wish to sketch in the coming pages of the architecture profession—as not yet fully bleak, but intermittently so; certainly not a lost cause but so long adrift that drifting has come to feel normal—is not its inevitable future. To help it regain its inner compass and reassert its purpose to the world is the purpose of this book. The argument to be defended here is that *the best hope for the profession of architecture to justify itself ethically is in the net public good that emanates from its protected status.* I try to demonstrate that the ethical grounding for the architecture profession in the public good it achieves is actually the logical realization, or the coming together at last, of events and concepts that both drew on the logic of the Enlightenment and furthered it. At their best, they are intimately woven with middle-class values—"the bourgeois ethics," in Diedre McCloskey's memorable terminology—that exist in deep hostility to the aristocratic attitudes that all we too readily excuse. These events and concepts—the event of capitalism itself, the modern concept of the professions, and the concept of the public—all are realizations of the great enrichment begun in the eighteenth century and they make sense together. And so, the work of this book is to explore architecture's relation to an expanded understanding of the public and make propositions regarding how a new conception of the public good could help us understand, explain, and solidify the profession's standing with it, with the ultimate goal of helping to substantiate why architecture is and should continue to be a protected profession. While I hope that the basic sensibility of this proposal has intuitive appeal, it turns out that the questions of "Who is the Public," and "What is its Good?" are far from simple and will require several steps to get to a satisfactory assertion concerning architects' role in it.

Chapter 2
THE ARCHITECTURE PROFESSION IN CAPITALISM

The professional practice of architecture is embedded in, indeed is a creature of, the capitalist economic system. This does not mean that it doesn't sometimes exist in tension with capitalism, but it does mean that it was only made possible by the rise of capitalism. This chapter will discuss four different sources of tension between the profession and capital: the divergence between economic and cultural dominance within the profession itself; the inability of the profession to fully monetize good design; growing tensions both within and outside the profession resulting from rising income inequality; and the stresses between economic globalization and resistant cultures which reverberate through the architecture profession.

One source of tension between architecture and capitalism is that in architecture, economic dominance and cultural dominance mostly diverge. The largest, richest architecture firms are unlikely to be the artistic leaders. This is not always the case in the arts. In television, in the movies, as well as in certain genres of music, financial success and cultural import are more closely aligned. Indeed, in fields where they diverge, like architecture, financial success breeds suspicion of having lost one's edge. Even though economic dominance is suspect in the architecture field, supporters of the primacy of artistic accomplishment often want it to be true that artistic success pays. In essence, they wish to hold on to the existence of a one-way direction of influence: from cultural artistic achievement to financial success, but not the reverse. There is no solid evidence for this view, and much points to its opposite: that no correlation exists, or a negative correlation exists, between artistic success and economic success in architecture. I want to first explain why the positive correlation view is wrong, and then assert that the lack of correlation between artistic and financial success is to be expected, and that we should consider this a good thing.

The professional practice of architecture is a middle-class phenomenon. In fact, it is triply indebted to the middle class: The professions, as we know

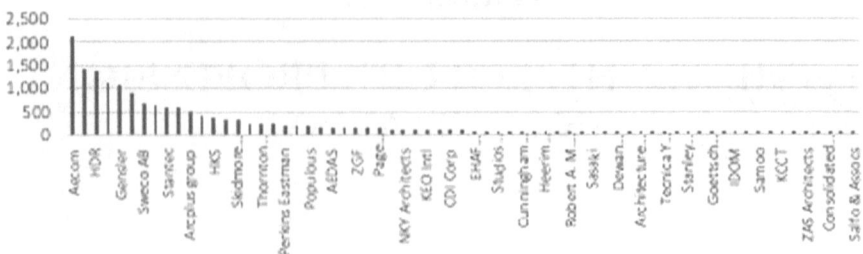

Figure 2.1 2016 Revenues for the largest architecture firms
Source: Tom Spector

them, are a manifestation of the rise of the bourgeois public in the eighteenth century. Their practitioners can realistically aspire to a middle-class existence, and much of their outlook derives from middle-class values. And yet, these selfsame sources of the profession's public, its viability, and its justification are in retreat in modern times. Recent developments in global capitalism and sheer demographics point to the disintegration of architecture's own middle class in favor of a refeudalization or at least the industrialization of architectural production. Even before economic globalization hit its current stride the architecture profession cultivated ambivalence toward the bourgeois ethics by promoting the extremes of an aristocratic–patron orientation on one side of the middle class in images it chose to extoll while its manifestos nurtured a proletarian–avant-gardist program on the other side of the middle. In the middle was the bourgeois bogeyman.

Although the values underlying both the professions and the public are bourgeois in derivation, the professions' relationship to capitalism differs from that of the public. Professions are a way in which occupations seek to insulate themselves from the extreme highs and lows of capitalist expansion, contraction and competition, while simultaneously asserting a certain status in society. The concept of the public, however, was more of an ideological weapon first employed by the rising bourgeoisie to wrest, first, moral authority and then political power from the church and the aristocracy. Neither the materialistic intentions underlying the professions nor the bourgeois origins underlying the concept of the public automatically make them somehow nefarious. The promotion of both occupational professionalism as well as the public can be morally sound, if done for the right reasons.

Now that capitalism strides the globe ascendant, architects have begun and must continue to learn to work with it. There is much evidence to suggest that architects in general are considerably better businesspersons than they were 50 years ago. As a whole, despite some real pain, firms weathered the Great Recession with fewer bankruptcies than in previous recessions. Furthermore, after many flat decades, productivity increases are starting to be in evidence with the efficiencies made possible by BIM and other technologies. The socialistic hopes of one of the tent poles of modernism—that the state will fund large-scale interventions in the market for architects' good works: works which help people live dignified existences, works which attack human-caused global warming, works which bring together people of all socioeconomic backgrounds—appear to have been dashed for good in the late 1980s. Capitalism won; socialism has been dead and gone for some thirty years. It's capitalism 24/7, 365 days of the year now, and that's just the situation we must work within. Perhaps those dashed hopes are a good riddance. As Chapter 1 introduces and as is discussed more thoroughly below, architects' disdain for capitalism generally serves to provide cover for treating people poorly.

A state-sanctioned profession, like architecture as it is practiced in most of the developed world, works to defeat the extreme highs and lows of capitalism through restricting the supply of credentialed professionals and creating limited monopolies over demand. By defeating, if only in limited ways, the vagaries of the marketplace, professions would seem to be highly vulnerable to attack by the forces of neoliberal economics, but actually they turn out to be quite durable. For it turns out that, especially in highly urbanized cultures, the professions provide some respite from the uncertainty of hiring a stranger as a service provider for matters of critical importance—preserving your health, keeping you out of jail, or designing your larger buildings, for example. This respite has some real market value. Even though a profession creates a dampening effect on the marketplace for goods and services, it dares not dampen things too much, for then its legitimacy will come into question. And so, the architecture profession must work within capitalism, for, what else is there? But, at the same time, the profession gets to modify capitalism a little bit with a degree of control over the market for its services.

Professions help alleviate two essential problems endemic to capitalism. In the first case, the market only works efficiently when both sides to a transaction have the full information they need to make informed decisions. But, deciding on a course of medical treatment, or solving a legal problem, or commissioning a public building require significantly more knowledge than it is reasonable to expect the average person to have. The problem of unequal and incomplete information due to the highly technical nature of the knowledge required is addressed by the professions through impartial credentialing—a kind of shorthand for determining that a practitioner has at least the minimum training and skill needed to provide the service at hand. In the second problem, the market may be poor at addressing externalities in matters of high importance. In other words, market mechanisms have limited ability to account for the widespread misery of infectious diseases, air and water pollution, climate change, the social breakdown that emanates from injustice, and the dangers and long-term suffering caused by poorly designed buildings. And so professions, despite their inefficiencies (Have you tried to schedule a dermatology appointment lately?) are creatures of capitalism. In the long run, when done right, they help capitalism function better by helping to provide important information about the service provider and by helping reduce hard-to-model risks. When done for spurious reasons, they create purely self-serving monopolies that breed large market inefficiencies.

Good Design Is *Not* Good Business

Architects' historic desire to assert the value of their work has taken on a sense of urgency in recent times. What was traditionally only a low-level concern has become acute for several reasons:

- The disrepute of the modernist/functionalist promise of improving the world through the modernist idioms of clean lines, mechanical imagery, advanced technology, and material efficiency left architecture without a dominant ethic.
- The apparent triumph of the market economy throughout the world as the only viable mechanism for insuring anything like the efficient distribution of goods and services places pressure on architecture to justify itself in economic terms.
- The penetration of consumer ideals into the government and other aspects of the public realm has also reached architecture.
- The increasing marginality of traditional architectural practice due to the disrepute of the modernist paradigm, as well as to the business pressures emplaced by the rise of such competing providers as design/build contractors, construction managers, and interior designers has called into question the value to society of the continuing existence of the profession.

The American Institute of Architects (AIA) has responded to these pressures with diverse initiatives; the longest running of which is to promote an image of the architect as someone whose activities make a crucial contribution to the business bottom line. This image has been promoted in television advertisements funded by the AIA as well as in a specially devised annual awards program entitled "Good Design is Good Business" begun in 1997 by the AIA's official publication at the time, *Architectural Record*, in conjunction with its sister magazine at McGraw-Hill, *Business Week*. This awards program recognizes exemplary contributions made by buildings to both beauty and to such business priorities as worker productivity, energy cost reduction, process efficiency, or maintenance cost reductions over what would be expected from "typical" or "ordinary" buildings. By embracing the consumer values of the market economy, the AIA has, in a single stroke, addressed the demand on the profession to justify itself according to capitalist priorities, the need to identify a dominant ethic, and reasserted the profession's centrality in the building process.

The AIA's assertion that architects should be more sophisticated about playing ball with business interests is long overdue but determining just how best to assert the market value of architecture is not a simple project. The more explicit one tries to become about just what sort of economic good architecture is, the more the complexity of its value becomes apparent. Yet, making explicit the types of value it offers is crucial, if its value to the market is to be asserted. The unequivocal economics of the marketplace demand that a good be classified as either a consumer good, a producer good, or an externality (something which is not measured).

As a consumer good, architecture provides people with objects, spaces, and experiences that they value. This valuing is reflected in what they are willing to pay for the good over and above what they are willing to pay for objects, spaces, and experiences of lesser design quality. As a consumer good, a work of architecture would ordinarily be subject to the law of diminishing marginal returns. Thus, the more of it is available, the less overall value one would attach to any given work. It has often been noted, however, that the economics of works of art do not work in precisely that way. Instead, the more one is exposed to paintings or classical music the more one demands of them, at least up to a point. Exposure to works of art leads one to become a more demanding and sophisticated consumer. This is in contrast to more standard consumer products like refrigerators. One can certainly become a connoisseur of good refrigerators, but after the purchase of one or two, the demand drops off quickly. Not so with items valued as works of art and other cultural goods. People may eagerly continue their purchases long after they've run out of display space to put them all. The quality level of their purchases can always be improved. The difference is that, unlike high-quality refrigerators, works of art are typically not fungible, one can't replace one with another and be just as satisfied (print-making being an exception to this rule). But this apparently inexhaustible valuing of works of art doesn't apply over and over to the same work. Instead, it applies to the valuing of works of art in general, or in series.

To any individual work of art, the consumption of its aesthetic value is still subject to exhaustion—to diminishing marginal returns. One can only consume the compositional lessons of Piet Mondrian's *Broadway Boogie-Woogie* so many times before becoming impatient to move on to other works.

In an important sense, then, the consumer model is inadequate. Yes, buildings can become obsolete, but this usually refers to functional, not aesthetic, obsolescence. The aesthetic value of individual buildings of high aesthetic merit is thought to be (at least within the profession) roughly inexhaustible, and this would seem to go against the consumer model. It may well be that this opinion of the timelessness of great buildings is a presumption in need of correction, but it should not be thrown away too quickly, for it forms an important part of many architects' overall outlook and is a strong motivator for their struggles to make the best buildings possible. It appears the consumer model of architectural value is at best a partial explanation of architecture's marketplace value; at worst it is simply misleading and counterproductive to the advocacy of good design, which traditionally strives to defeat time horizons. Though architects give much thought and attention to the needs of the users and owners of buildings, such persons are not usually looked on as consumers, in the sense of eventually using up the good provided. Instead, that use is usually considered to continue indefinitely in architects' design deliberations, even if it is well-understood that buildings require occasional updating. The consumer model suggests, contrary to this, that all buildings will have their day and that to maximize return and minimize the acquisition cost, this fact should be planned for. This is not the kind of design advocacy the AIA has in mind.

It appears that the AIA and *Business Week* have more in mind an idea of architecture as a producer good in its awards program. As a producer good, architecture can positively impact the bottom line in a myriad of ways: it may allow work processes to occur more efficiently; it may improve employee satisfaction and thereby reduce expensive turnover and job-related illness; or it may give a business a marketing edge by helping it establish a certain desired image with consumers. Producer goods aren't consumer goods because they are instruments of continued productivity. Architecture, in this scenario, becomes a business tool alongside new machinery, stock-option plans, and advertising campaigns. Despite the enduring appeal of machine aesthetics in the profession, the hazard of this avenue of justification is obvious. Treating design quality entirely as a business strategy falls far short of demonstrating the kind and level of value the AIA is seeking to show in the awards program and threatens to devalue the cause of architecture. The desire to build well and the desire to maximize profit may not be identical. The AIA is not seeking to show business that good design is an idea to be manipulated for maximum profit, but rather, to show that building well and beautifully is not incompatible with business motives; that the pursuit of exemplary design, in addition to being a worthy motive in itself, also has tangible collateral benefits to business because the elements of good design facilitate the realization of universally held human needs and desires. The AIA would like to treat the desire to build well and beautifully as a set of intentions that originate, in necessary part, external to marketplace considerations, but to have its awards program demonstrate that this desire just also happens to show positive bottom-line results. It wants to assert the one-directional relationship originating in artistically meritorious design and culminating in financial gain. It cannot allow good design to be portrayed only as a producer good, for that strikes at the heart of architects' design motivation as well as the very basis of the discipline's claims of professionalism. Once the cause of exemplary architectural design is given over *entirely* to the profit motive, the profession ceases to exist.

This approach makes good design out to be a hybrid good; one that originates necessarily in motives external to market economics (in part at least), but goods that may also serve profit motives as well. The idea that differing visions of the good go into the making of architecture, and that different (and possibly opposing) goods emerge from exemplary architectural design helps to capture the complexity of the relation of individual building with its urban situation. This paints a picture of a tense relationship between design motives internal and external to the market that should be discussed in a public forum at some point. However the problem of addressing this tense relationship will only arise if the AIA's claims to the market-friendly benefits of good design actually pan out.

Despite years of accumulation of the "Good Design Is Good Business" program's examples of buildings that improve the bottom line, the evidence of architecture's contribution to business priorities remains mostly anecdotal. Some solid economic research has been done on the subject but demonstrating the marketplace value of design excellence has turned out to be surprisingly difficult. Three studies by economists in recent decades have sought to address the question of the value of good design in the marketplace. The general drift of these findings is far from providing solid backup for the AIA's claims but they may at least suggest potentially more durable and resonant directions for those seeking to bolster the cause of excellence in architecture.

Economic Studies of Design Profitability

In the late 1970s in Chicago, and in the mid-1980s and again in the early 1990s in Boston, economic researchers attempted to uncover any correlations that might exist between superior design in office buildings and profitability.

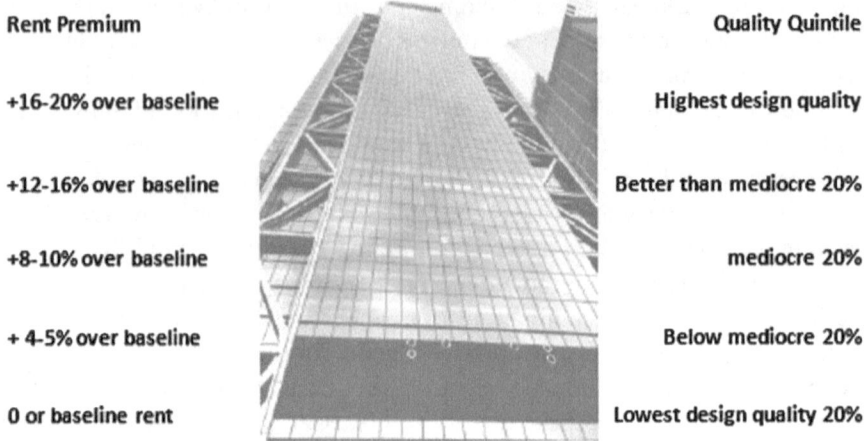

Figure 2.2 Rents increase as design quality increases in commercial office buildings
Source: Tom Spector

By "superior design" the researchers meant something like "aesthetically superlative" or "more beautiful." In Chicago, Douglas Hough and Charles Kratz examined rental data from 139 office buildings that had either been determined to be landmarks (for pre-1930s buildings) or had received design awards from the Chicago chapter of the AIA (for post–World War II buildings). They then compared the financial performance of this group of buildings with the general population of office buildings. The economists concluded that a substantial rent premium (22 percent above average) is attributable to recent buildings (post-1950) of recognized architectural aesthetic quality, but that no premium accrues to landmark historic buildings.

In a follow-up study, economist Kerry Vandell and his researchers considered 102 Class A office buildings in the Boston Area. These buildings were ranked for overall design quality by 28 surveyed architects. This approach allowed the researchers to divide the buildings up into quintiles of overall design quality. Their results confirmed one aspect of the Hough study: that buildings rated in the top quintile for quality could be predicted to garner almost 22 percent higher rents than those rated in the bottom quintile. In between, rents increased approximately 4–5 percent between each quintile. Both of these studies anticipated that a cost premium would also associate itself with good design, but both went on to calculate that the cost premium would not absorb all the rental premium: that is to say, that it was a profitable move to design to quality.

So far, this is all encouraging to the AIA's efforts.

Both Hough and Vandell thought their findings raised several questions. Hough wondered why, if the profitability of good design was so apparent, weren't developers and owners of office buildings lining up for more of it? After all, developers are reasonably smart and, certainly, greedy people not prone to leaving money on the table. He suggested the following explanations: The first likely explanation for the apparent lack of interest in this route to exceeding market expectations is that the pursuit of architectural quality may operate for its owners as something of a lottery. That is, as Douglas E. Hough and Charles G. Kratz put it, "although clients can improve the odds by selecting particular architects, they cannot guarantee the quality of the product."[1] Favorable judgment of architectural quality is invariably dependent on novelty and originality, and the pursuit of these attributes is inherently risky. Therefore, this route to business success would not attract the risk averse. Thus, the rent premium "may represent nothing more than the risk premium necessary to compensate owners for gambling on architectural quality."[2] In other words, just because one aims for architecture of aesthetic distinction doesn't mean that it will be achieved; even hiring the most blue-ribbon architect cannot assure such an outcome. Hough's second explanation is related to the first in the observation that there is, at any given time, only a relatively small pool of architects able to provide such design quality. Given the changing nature of tastes and the market, the abilities of even this small pool to keep up the quality production level may have a limited career span. (Indeed, Judith R. Blau demonstrated that one decade's award-winning firms are seldom the next decade's—thus adding to the risk of aesthetic failure.[3])

Vandell concurred with Hough's lottery conclusion, but was even more pessimistic about the profitability conclusion. He thought the increased risk associated with the pursuit of aesthetic excellence was sufficiently high that the pursuit of good design did not actually lead to increased profitability on average; it only led to increased profitability for a few of those who took the risk and won—that is to say, actually produced aesthetically meritorious buildings. Indeed, Vandell lays out the bitter conclusion for architects that profitability is "predicted to actually decline on average with increases in design quality" due to increased expense and risk.[4] Vandell also concurred with Hough's finding that the age of a building plays an important role in its perceived design merit and demonstrated most convincingly that there is such a thing as aesthetic obsolescence when it comes to measuring the benefits of good design in the market: The rent premiums associated with older, higher rated buildings flatten out with age. Furthermore, consensus judgment of a building's design quality tends to diminish with its age as well. In conclusion, Vandell noted that these results were only reflective of a certain set of market conditions: a rental market in which absorption is strong and vacancy is low. Whether the

Figure 2.3 Chicago skyline
Source: Tom Spector

correlation they found would hold in less hospitable market conditions was unknown.

Vandell sought to correct this particular hole in the data by studying the same market five years later during the recession that saw a marked weakening in demand for office space in the Boston area market. This study found that during weak markets no discernible difference in rents between high- and low-rated buildings could be isolated: The rental premium for aesthetic quality

Figure 2.4 Boston Towers
Source: Tom Spector

evaporates. The researchers did report, however, the encouraging results that the top quintile buildings in aesthetic quality sustained lower vacancy rates than low-rated buildings during this period; a development that, of course, positively affected profitability.[5]

Design Obsolescence

The Vandell and Hough studies bring up two vexing issues confronting architects wishing to emphasize the economic value of good design. The first issue stems from the observation that the judgment of design quality, and the resulting perceived worth of buildings, so obviously declines over time. This may tend to support the idea of architecture as a consumer good in addition to its production value. Architects have reason to think that just the opposite should be the case and that it would be good that it was the case. Though these studies lack a longitudinal view of the fate of attitudes toward the design merit of any specific building, they do, unequivocally, point toward a declining estimation of aesthetic merit in general as buildings age. The idea of what Vandell casually calls "design obsolescence" but what we should, given the nature of his inquiry, more precisely call aesthetic merit obsolescence, ought to be a particularly troubling one for architects. Not only do architects cherish the notion that their opinions on such matters are durable and based on timeless principles, but they stake a lot on the idea that buildings gracing their urban environments over the years—as they age and fit in—actually increase in esteem. The idea of the convergence of received historical judgment is an idea in which anyone in the arts places great stock. These results suggest an utter lack of convergence. It may be that the so-called convergence of artistic opinion isn't sustained without a whole lot of coercion in the form of unquestioned dogma and carefully framed choices.

Those disturbed by the apparent erosion (in contrast to the expected consolidation) of consensus opinion might argue that even the time frame of 60 years or so is too short to separate the wheat from the chafe. There is, after all, the well-known phenomenon of each generation feeling compelled to reject its immediate predecessors' values. This might be true, but it can only explain so much. To say that Vandell's and Hough's data is misleading because it just doesn't go back far enough dismisses the matter too easily. How far back must we look? After all, a modernist rejection of history held sway for quite some time, certainly more than a generation. But even if there is some truth to the generation-skipping argument, it would seem that some buildings from the rejected generation ought to slip through. (Much like the Crystal Palace slipped through the condemnation of the rest of the

Victorian period by the early modernists.) There may be evidence of this somewhere, but the Vandell and Hough studies neither show nor suggest it. If the consensus over design merit is ephemeral and reverses itself in the span of 10–20 years, then not only do clients have less reason to take a risk on pursuing superior design quality, there is little reason for architects wishing to be on the side of lasting value to give aesthetic consideration much weight in their calculations either. Lasting value may have more to do with a building's physical durability, and its ability to accommodate economically valued activities, than with *venustas*. Those in it for the long term may have to reorient their thinking, or else admit a closer relationship between design quality and fashion than they care to.

These studies also raise the question of whether architects are in the best position to judge aesthetic merit. In the art world, this function is usually left to critics and patrons and the interested public, not to the artists themselves. What would have happened to the correlation if, say, architecture critics, urban designers, art lovers, or just a sample of the well-educated populace did the choosing? Might the correlation be even stronger? We just don't know. The advantage of using architects as the judges of aesthetic superiority is that they, after all, as the chief providers have a significant role in determining what the built environment actually looks like. Therefore, architects' judgments of aesthetic merit are likely to be both prescient for the eventual appearance of the built environment, as well as influential regarding at least what will be available in the way of meritorious buildings to choose from. But from this privileged position as providers, it does not follow that architects are in critically privileged position as judges.

Risk

The second issue these studies bring to the fore centers on the subject of risk. The problematic relationship between aesthetic quality and profitability identified in these studies may well be even more risky than is contemplated by their authors, for neither set of researchers tried to measure or isolate a group of buildings conspicuous as business failures. This omission constitutes a major limitation of these studies. The world of architecture is studded with examples of clients whose enthusiasm for design excellence played a role in their slide to a precarious financial status or outright ruin. An unscientifically chosen list of high-profile examples would include such diverse entities as the IBM Corporation, Lloyds of London, the City of New York, the real estate developers Olympia and York, and the American Center in Paris. In each case, these organizations became known as significant patrons of architecture immediately before their organizations reached or tottered on the edge of failure. Those that survived did so in part by discarding their architectural ambitions as part of their survival strategy. Should anything be made of such a selectively chosen list?

The distinct possibility is that these organizations' preoccupation with design quality may have either led important decision makers to become distracted from the actual operation of the business, or that allocating the extra capital required to pursue architectural quality emaciates the organization of assets much-needed to remain competitive in the market. Thus Hough's and Vandell's lottery description may work in the opposite direction too: not only may one not achieve the profitability sought, the pursuit of aesthetic excellence just may increase the potential for catastrophic results—results much worse than would have occurred if these organizations had set their sights on a lower mark.

The most important lesson to come from these studies for architects wishing to demonstrate the value of aesthetic merit is that they make explicit an intimate connection between pursuit of design quality and risk—a connection that is often merely implied or even buried in architects' ideals. The risks take several forms:

- A cost premium associated with pursuing aesthetic quality is likely.
- It may be easier to not only not to achieve one's goals, but also to reach catastrophic failure.
- The pursuit of aesthetic excellence may result in unusual designs which alienate more people than would a more moderate course.
- The pursuit of aesthetic excellence may tend to divert owners from paying attention to other (and possibly more pressing) bottom-line issues.

These considerations combined may take the increased risk associated with pursuing aesthetic excellence to intolerable heights for all but the most ardent gamblers.

The Vandell studies suggest the conclusion that a better correlation between design and profitability is likely to be found in the middle quintiles than in the top quintiles. Against the hypothesis that a strong correlation exists between profitability and the pursuit of design excellence, it would not be much of a leap to read these studies as suggesting that a better correlation exists between profitability and the pursuit of slightly-better-than-mediocre design. At the slightly-above-mediocre stage, risk (aesthetic, cost, and diverted attention) is minimized, while the potential benefits of bettering the market average for both rental and vacancy rates are still in place: In good markets, one can expect a slightly-better-than-mediocre building to perform 5 percent better than those just below the middle quintile, while the risk of aesthetic failure and the long steep slide toward aesthetic obsolescence is almost nonexistent because the results are mostly predictable. The results are predictable from an aesthetic standpoint because the design doesn't stray too far from the known. They are predictable from a business standpoint because the cost and technological risks are slight; the precedents are plentiful. Finally, the results are predictable because slightly-better-than-mediocre buildings are unlikely to occupy huge chunks of the owner's and developer's attention. Thus, it would seem that the AIA and *Architectural Record* would be on much firmer ground with the slogan "slightly better than mediocre design is good business," but of course both organizations would be loath to boast such a thing, despite the fact that this level of design does, in fact, seem to be exactly what developers and owners are lining up for. Owners and clients are lining up for slightly-better-than-mediocre because owners and developers, while greedy, are also capable of assessing risk. They know that the greater the risk, the more likely they are to suffer for their decisions.

Public and Private Goods

It seems plausible to conclude, therefore, that the attempt to establish a profit motive for pursuing exemplary design not only cannot be demonstrated in any convincing way, as the economists' studies show, but even more to the point, simply is an undesirable tactic altogether. Even *Architectural Record* may be backing off from these claims: Winners of this awards program have included a preschool, a museum, a business that failed before it even moved in, and even a Zen Buddhist retreat (surely the antithesis of the profit motive).[6] If these users and these structures can be examples of how design can be good for business, then the program, one could reasonably argue, has lost its distinctiveness from any other awards program.

If the economic rationality of good design cannot be demonstrated, and if the desirability of attempting to do so is in doubt anyway, but architects still have the conviction that the pursuit of the exemplary is preferable to the pursuit of the slightly-above-mediocre, where should they turn for justification? How do they go about reestablishing a dominant design ethic, promoting the value of building well and beautifully, and shoring up the importance of the profession? I want to suggest that the rationale for design that goes above and beyond profit motives lies in the market externalities. These externalities—invisible to the market but crucial in a life well lived—are what justify the existence of providers somewhat insulated from the market.

The differences in approach are fundamental. The business orientation promoted by the AIA and *Architectural Record* enjoys the built-in widespread assent of society by piggybacking on existing means and systems of consumption. It seeks to describe the good of architecture as so many private goods which, when bundled together in a market economy, create the public good of more, better, and more efficiently delivered consumer choices. This argument is drawn from classical economics in which the good of the many is said to be achieved by individuals' pursuit of self-interest. It would not be unreasonable to postulate that the marketplace would therefore favor things which can be consumed in individual, self-interested transactions. It is easy to see that the good of superior architectural merit would be resistant to being fully consumed in that way, and hence would fare poorly in the estimation of the marketplace.

An alternative orientation would seek to ground architectural value instead as a public good, and only indirectly as a private good. The AIA and *Architectural Record* could, then, seek sensible ways to extend the idea of public welfare to include protection from built environments that are not only likely to topple and kill, but are also harsh, ugly, and insensitive to a wide range of human needs, including the needs of those indirectly affected by them. The cause of aesthetic merit has an important place in such a conception. It is impossible to conceive of environments as hospitable, without thinking of them in aesthetic terms.

Asserting the importance of good design as a market externality is not to retreat into a disengaged elitism but it does emphasize the limitations of the market approach. Human goods that require public participation to be goods, such as city parks, fresh air, vaccinations against pandemics, and national security are notoriously underserved by the marketplace even though each one may well favorably impact business profitability. Is it too much of a stretch to consider architecture one of those goods and therefore the architecture profession as the rightful delivery mechanism?

Admittedly, these arguments against the business orientation promoted by the AIA make some broad generalizations from a few studies of the marketplace value of design excellence. Accordingly, this interpretation is forwarded less as a conclusive finding than as a caution and a plausible alternative to the claims made by the proponents of the business orientation; claims which ultimately rest on anecdotal evidence and unjustified interpretations of economic research. The assertion of architecture as primarily a public good may not be a panacea for the project of reasserting a strong role for architecture in the world, but it seems, at least, a worthy successor and alternative to the one we have now, even though it does leave open the question of how it creates a positive public benefit in the midst of an increasingly privatized civic realm, a question I will examine in Chapter 5.

Globalization and the Waning of the Architectural Middle Class

Though the architecture profession is both a creation of and a beneficiary of capitalist society, this does not mean that we are therefore obligated to welcome uncritically all its manifestations. Globalization is a case in point. Globalization has a fundamental impact on the rise in income inequality in developed nations (even as it precipitates a rise in overall income globally) and on developed nations' inability to do anything about it. These processes affect the architecture profession in ways which impact both its fundamental structure as well as its bargain with the public. French economist Thomas Piketty, in his landmark book *Capital in the 21st Century*, provides the basis for an explanation of the mechanisms at work by separating the fruits of labor income from that of investment income. Piketty explains that there are two and only two basic sources of income in a capitalist society: labor earnings, and investments. The sources of labor earnings are probably obvious. Anyone who obtains a salary or income from work: whether an NBA basketball player, a stockbroker with a large Wall Street investment house, an actor, or a lowly architectural intern is earning money based on their labor. It is easy to see how a manager or corporate CEO, whose earnings can be defined as a percent of the earnings of each employee's they manage, benefit when the number of employees in a corporation grows. Increases in labor are primarily what justifies increases in management salaries in labor-heavy industries such as architectural services.

Investment earnings capable of earning income derive from agricultural land, housing, stock investments, loans to others, and machinery and equipment of all kinds. In addition to capitalist earnings, governments can transfer earnings from one individual to another—but these transfers do not directly increase the overall economic product of any given economy—they just move the money around that is earned elsewhere. Year in and year out, over long projections, capital investments can be seen to earn between 4–5 percent annually. This rate of return is denoted by Piketty as (r).

Developing economies, like China and India, may exceed a 4–5 percent economic growth rate (G) but mature capitalist economies rarely grow this fast. The United States, for example, usually grows at the rate of 2.2–2.5 percent. Europe has been doing much worse: European countries are in the .5 percent to 1.5 percent range. During the 1950s, the US growth rate swung widely—from negative 1 percent to over 8 percent, but averaged over 5 percent. By contrast, India grew at a 10 percent rate in 2010 and 7.4 percent in 2012. China achieved something similar in the 1990s and the 2000s. (Keep in mind that, if an economy grows at a 7 percent annual rate, then because of compounding, in only 10 years the size of that economy has doubled.) This pace of growth is very hard to sustain. Once most people in the economy are employed in industrial labor and basic infrastructure is installed, then growth is mostly dependent on either entering new markets or else technological leaps leading to productivity gains.

It is hard for labor earnings to increase faster than the overall economy without being inflationary. This is another reason that globalization is attractive: It lets management reach out beyond their domestic economies for growth. If increases in labor earnings lead to higher inflation, then they tend to cancel each other out. If investments typically earn 4–5 percent year in and year out, and labor earnings can only grow at the rate of the growth of any given country's GDP, then r > G most of the time. Therefore, the share of the national income going to investment earnings over labor earnings can be predicted to increase over time. This basic fact is what leads to economic inequality in advanced capitalist societies. Piketty shows that this is exactly what has been happening since the 1970s. Slowly and inexorably, the value of private capital as a percent of national income in the United States (or GDP) has been increasing, from 350 percent in 1970 to over 400 percent, even after the recession wiped out a reserve of wealth, in 2010. Even in more redistributive nations such as Germany, the value of private wealth has been in a steady climb during this period, from just over 200 percent of GDP in 1970 to over 400 percent today. What does that capital consist of? Agricultural land, the nation's housing stock, other capital investments, and a very small net of foreign investment. This increase is the function r—G = net rate of increase on the value of investment capital as a percent of national capital.[7]

Now, there is nothing wrong with people saving and increasing the value of their capital investments. It is beneficial to the overall economy that people should do so. It helps enable future growth. But here is where it becomes worrisome: If the bottom 50 percent of society owns almost no productive or valuable capital, then over time the national income is going to skew in favor of the already rich. Going back to the nineteenth century, European countries had an extreme concentration of wealth at the top. About 90 percent of Europe's aggregate wealth belonged to the top 10 percent, while 60 percent of the wealth belonged to just the top 1 percent! This concentration was highly diluted during the twentieth century due to two world wars, the Great Depression, and highly redistributive tax rates following World War II.

Today the concentration of wealth in the United States is not what it was at the end of the nineteenth century. About 60–70 percent of the wealth is controlled by the top 10 percent. The bottom 50 percent still owns almost nothing, but the middle class owns 20–30 percent of the national wealth. However, the share of total earnings by the top 10 percent or top decile, is actually *greater* now than it was in the nineteenth century. As a result, the middle-class's share of the nation's income is shrinking. What was once the envy of the world is a lead that is fast disappearing relative to other developed nations. It appears that Canada has now taken the lead in the middle-class's share of national income. We can see evidence of this growing disparity in the growth in the wealth of billionaires worldwide versus the growth in the number of billionaires. Between 1987 and 2013, the average growth at the very top of the economic heap has been 6.7 percent, while the average world wealth has grown only 2.1 percent. The rich are getting richer and the superrich are getting super-richer. When it is said that the United States has become more unequal than Europe, that statistic can be misleading. It needs to be investigated a bit. The percentage of wealth owned by the rich is still noticeably less than in Europe, but, in the United States, the growth in labor income for the superrich has far outpaced that of Europe. The upshot being that when you put the two together—investment income + labor income— you get a more unequal society.

This trend has been accelerated by US government policy cutting the highest tax rates, which function as government transfers to the rich. Following World War II, US tax rates were as high as 90 percent in the highest income strata to help the government pay for the war. But these have been falling into the 30 percent range today, with corporate taxes having been reduced still further in 2017. The same applies to inheritance taxes. While marginal tax rates have been progressively lowered and the federal debt has climbed, the wage-earning jobs have become progressively skewed toward low-wage occupations. While 22 percent of the job losses during the Great Recession were in what is classified as low-wage occupations, 44 percent of the job gains since the Recession have been in that category. That means that most of the job gains since the recession have been in jobs that will not lead to growth of the middle class.

This observation squares with statistics showing the disparity between income growth between the top 10 percent and the bottom 90 percent since the recession. Although a 2011 Congressional Budget Office (CBO) report demonstrated that real net *average* US household income grew 62 percent from 1979 to 2007, the household income growth was much more rapid at the higher end of the income scale than at the middle and lower ends. In 1979, the bottom four-fifths of the income spectrum earned nearly 60 percent of total labor income, about 33 percent of income from capital and business, and about 8 percent from capital gains. By 2007, the bottom four-fifths share of labor income had dropped to less than 50 percent, the income from capital and business had decreased to 20 percent, and capital gains fell to about 5 percent. In other words, all sources of income were less evenly distributed in 2007 than in 1979. Revisiting the issue in 2013, the CBO showed that after-tax average income soared 15.1 percent for the top 1 percent from 2009 to 2010, but grew by less than 1 percent for the bottom 90 percent over the same time period, and fell for many income groups. These trends continued during the 2010s.[8]

While labor income accounted for nearly three-fourths of market income in the United States from 1979 to 2007, that figure had dropped to two-thirds by 2007. Capital income (excluding capital gains) is the next largest source, but even at its 1981 peak, it represented only 14 percent of total market income before falling to about 10 percent of total income in 2007. Conversely, income from capital gains rose, doubling to approximately 8 percent of the market income in 2007 from about 4 percent in 1979. Business income and income from other sources (primarily private pensions) each accounted for about 7 percent of the total income in 2007, up from about 4 percent each.

The architecture profession is not immune to these same globalization trends. We need to look at what's going on from two directions: from the direction of changes in the market for architectural services, and from the direction of changes within the structure of the profession itself. Here is how the economic trends in society at large are mirrored in what's happening in the architectural and engineering professions.

The difference between mean CEO salaries and entry-level salaries in architecture is not nearly as skewed as it is in many other occupations. The average architecture firm CEO makes only three times what an intern makes, while in large corporations across the economy CEOs average *300* times what the average worker makes in that company. (This is up from 20x back in 1965.) The Bureau of Labor Statistics estimates that architectural and engineering managers average what would be considered upper middle-class incomes in the $130,000 range, while experienced interns can expect to make in the $50,000+ range. Not a huge disparity considering what has happened in the economy as a whole.

But the trend toward consolidation of the architectural and engineering business into fewer, larger and more economically dominant firms is pronounced. The graph in Figure 2.1 of the incomes from the top two hundred A+E firms in the United States, shows an incredibly steep slope that quickly levels off, indicating that a few really large firms are soaking up the lion's share of the income.

The top five firms (AECOM, NORR, HDR, DAR Group, and Gensler) generated nearly $7.2 billion in revenue from AE services in 2016. It takes the next 20 to generate the same amount, and the remaining 42 on the chart generate only $2.24 billion. Top-ranked AECOM continues to distance itself from the pack. AECOM's 2018 total revenue topped $ 20 billion, up from 18.2 billion in 2017, with design and consulting services providing 40 percent,

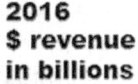
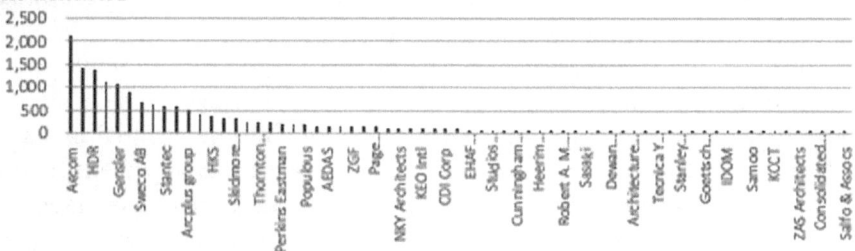

Figure 2.5 Globalized AE revenues, 2016
Source: Tom Spector

or roughly $8 billion of that revenue. AECOM's force of 87,000 employees rivals the size of the AIA's, which has 95,000 members.[9]

In Appendix B, we see that just the top 20 firms, out of some 20,000 + architecture firms in the Unites States are estimated to have generated some 42 percent of the market share. Continuing consolidation is a trend showing no sign of slowing. In a recent poll, most architecture firms are considering mergers or acquisitions. This trend portends a further widening of the income disparity between architectural management and labor. While the industry's mega-firms in the top 500 have added an average $3.05 billion per company to their value between 1986 and 2011, midsize firms have only been able to increase their revenue by an average of $16 million per company during the same period. As a result, it is estimated that the mega-firms increased their percentage of total industry revenue from 10 percent in 1986 to 41 percent in 2011, taking some of that volume from the large and midsize firms. The merely large and midsize firms have lost 12 percent and 21 percent of their relative income since peaking in 1986.[10]

The processes of globalization reflect what has been happening with income growth in the workforce as well. While, happily, growth of entry-level and midlevel architectural and engineering incomes has been much better than in the overall economy in the 2010s, growth in those income levels is dwarfed by the growth in incomes at the managerial level. The first reason for this growing disparity is obvious. If you were the leader of a 15-person firm and suddenly you are the leader of a 30-person firm, your income is going to increase. For every dollar earned by direct labor in the production of work in an architecture firm, less than half goes to pay the person's salary. The remainder goes to overhead expenses like rent, utilities, materials, software, furnishings, and to marketing and management. If, say, management gleans 10 percent of every dollar brought in the door then if the same management is gleaning 10 percent of 100 people, rather than 50, it stands to reason that management salaries will increase substantially.

But the other reasons that might be driving the increase in upper management salaries relative to the interns and less experienced workers are the increases in productivity and increased profits from investment and from international work. Indeed, worker productivity in large firms is 60 percent greater than in small firms.[11] Of the $10 trillion worldwide construction industry, 12 percent is in the United States. Thus, firms positioned for international work are poised to capture much greater percentages of the total work just by virtue of riding the wave.[12]

The upshot is that the profession is becoming increasingly bifurcated into the large (hundreds of employees and multiple offices), and the super large (thousands of employees and globally distributed offices) on the one hand, and numerous boutique-sized firms (one office, less than twenty employees) on the other. The architectural middle class (one or two offices, less than one hundred employees) is getting squeezed out of existence. How does this matter to the project here of reasserting the good of the profession?

While employees of globalized firms and employees of boutique-sized firms are both likely to count themselves as part of the global economic middle class (although employees of large firms do earn more than those of small firms) what neither is able to take part of is the middle-class value of ownership—in the mega firms, because only a small fraction of the thousands of employees will ever be owners, and in the boutique firms, because there is so little to own. It's in the space in the middle where chances for advancement, growth, upper management and partnership are at their greatest. And so, even though within the world economy practicing architects can still count on reaching the economic middle class, what has become much tougher to count on is that, *within* the profession of architecture there will much of a middle. Increasingly, there is labor, and there are owners. This matters because the middle class—the bourgeoisie—is not just about a range of income but has also always been defined by a set of values: The meritocracy, advancement through hard work, and participating in ownership of one's work, livelihood and profession. But, as the title of the article "The 50-Year-old Intern Architect" suggests, for many those aspirations have dwindled to nothing.[13]

Globalization and Moral Relativism

Economic globalization without cultural globalization is bound to create dilemmas for well-meaning Western architects in international practices.

International corporations will tend to seek out globalized practices for professional services. When this occurs, the international corporate client will, like as not, seek to proceed according to a world view of their ethical obligations that transcends that of any given jurisdiction. Since much action that gives moral concern stems from parochial national, regional, or tribal moral outlooks, this increasingly cosmopolitan orientation found in globalized work is welcome—unless the parochial outlook the multinationals are seeking to transcend runs roughshod over more local sensitivities and concerns. According to James R. Faulconbridge and Daniel Muzio,

> users are, then, increasingly asking professionals not to fulfil their role as it is defined and understood in their host national jurisdiction, but to operate globally and disconnected from national regimes whenever possible (Quack, 2007). Consequently, many GPSFs (global professional services firms) employ locally qualified and regulated professionals in every market they operate in but ask these professionals to adopt global standards of professional practice. [...] One approach developed by GPSFs is the design of strategies intended to allow the transcending of local versions of professionalism and the development of a cadre of truly global practitioners. [14]

This hopeful development, however, is not universally experienced by Western practitioners working overseas, who may experience pressures that seek to erode the values that an architect may have inculcated from his or her professional training. Inner moral conflict brought about by globalization occurs when working abroad within cultures that do not share our values or legal protections against, say, bribery, worker safety, environmental degradation, or theft of intellectual property. In such situations many architects—as philosopher Michael Zimmerman ably described in his essay "Globalization, Multiculturalism and Architectural Ethics" in Graham Owen's edited volume *Architecture, Ethics and Globalization*—feel torn between the undesirable poles of ethnocentric hubris or a stifling multicultural relativism.[15] Neither pole seems to provide the foundational certainty needed to establish firm ethical positions on these important matters. This situation—feeling the tug of latent conflicts within our Western Enlightenment-based values when confronted with the conflicting values of another culture—has become so dishearteningly commonplace in globalized architectural practice as to be gradually numbing to the values and sensitivities of the Western architect practicing abroad. Thomas Fisher, in the book *Ethics for Architects*, describes a related situation:

An internationally known architect received a commission to design a major public building for a government renowned for its repressiveness toward its own people and its aggressiveness toward neighboring countries. It would be an important project for the architect, although his peers criticized him for accepting the commission. The client has treated him well and has given him a great deal of latitude in the design of the project, and he has argued that doing a good building is his only ethical responsibility, regardless of what others think about the government's politics.[16]

Fisher's hypothetical (though, perhaps, thinly veiled) case calls to mind the real-world controversy between Martin Filler and Zaha Hadid over her stadium project in Qatar.[17] It also characterizes what has concerned other observers with her firm's work in Azerbaijan. The difference between the situation described by Zimmerman of the guilt-ridden architect concerned not to impose his values on another culture, and that described by Fisher of an architect largely unconcerned with the possibility of undermining his own values by working with repressive regimes is the same difference in type that we also saw between Rem Koolhaas's uncritical embrace of the power structures in Beijing and Lagos versus Daniel Libeskind's well-publicized disapproval he thinks should apply to those Western architects who choose to work under such conditions.[18] While both situations involve questions of the possible imposition of one culture's values on another's, they actually point to two distinctly different problems that architects grapple with under the umbrella terms of globalization and multiculturalism. The moral situation Fisher describes seems to be about the ethics of working in another culture as an opportunity to relax one's moral heritage in the name of multiculturalism, while the situation Zimmerman describes is of a practitioner hypersensitized and genuinely torn by what seem to be presented to him as conflicting prescriptions from within his own heritage for doing the right thing.

The humble, concerned architect in Zimmerman's account walks a fine line. He is striving not to let his own culture's values overwhelm his ability to arrive at a sensitive architectural solution but he also doesn't want to give over to such cultural commonplaces in international work as tribalism, denigration of women, nepotism, bribery, and disregard for environmental degradation. He doesn't want to find himself morally adrift, and yet he doesn't want to perpetuate some sort of ideological violence against another culture. His Enlightenment heritage tells him, among other things, that the ineliminable worth of the individual means that we should refrain from asserting our values on others who may well have different outlooks valid for them. How does he assert his ethical principles against such cultural commonplaces as nepotism without simultaneously asserting a version of Western cultural superiority, which he is loath to do? Conversely, can he possibly go along with these "traditions" without completely throwing over his own reasonably well-considered values? Farid Abdel-Nour diagnoses the problem succinctly thus: "This is the source of their guilt and discomfort. Their liberalism commits them not to engage in arbitrarily imposing standards on others, yet philosophy can no longer provide them with the blanket assurance that their use of liberal standards on nonliberals is not an arbitrary imposition."[19]

One possible way out of this dilemma, according to philosopher Richard Rorty, is to give up on the feeling that foundations are required in order to take an ethical stand. Rorty spent much of his career trying to disabuse the West of even the quest for certainty concerning its moral foundations. He said, in effect, the best we can and should hope for is solidarity. We can hope to bring in other people from other cultures into the Enlightenment tent with our bourgeois values, but if they don't share certain concepts, then we have no basis from which to appeal to them. We can reject their opposing views on, say, democracy, human rights, market economies, and the autonomy of art, but we are in no position to tell them that they are objectively wrong by doing so. Even so, he thinks, we have plenty of reason to argue for the preference of our ethnocentric Enlightenment bourgeois liberal values against other value systems. But Rorty doesn't think that we can objectively "prove" the superiority of this Western outlook to those who do not share enough of our culture to be convinced. Recognizing this limitation on our ability to convince others of the rightness of our value system—others who do not share our cultural heritage—Rorty argues that philosophers have unsuccessfully strived for 200 years or so to explain why Enlightenment morality (as found in such concepts as human rights) should be binding on everyone. Failing the establishment of a transcultural foundation for ethics, it seems that we must allow some sort of relativism. But, instead of falling into a defeatist cultural relativism, Rorty thinks we should opt for ethnocentrism. In *Objectivity, Relativism and Truth*, he writes: "I would hold that there is no truth in relativism, but this much truth in ethnocentrism: we cannot justify our beliefs (in physics, ethics or any other area) to everybody, but only to those whose beliefs overlap ours to some appropriate extent."[20] He goes on to say that this is not a theoretical problem but only a practical problem about the limits of argument. This conclusion, he believes, is neither a case of moral relativism nor must we allow that it is only hubris on our part.

Rorty forcefully criticized attempts to ground our Western commitment to human rights in anything essential in human nature—anything that stands outside of all cultures and all history—that is to say, a completely objective basis, or a God's-eye view. He thinks that attempts to ground human rights in, say, human rationality, have never worked and never will. "Human nature" certainly will not do. Human nature has as many deficiencies as it does bounties. "Human rationality" is not only always in short supply but also limited in explanatory power. "Human utility" rests on a subjectivity that that only serves to forestall the dilemma by a step. And, of course, recourse to a higher, nonhuman, power collapses the entire Enlightenment project in self-contradiction. Instead of feeling compelled to assert some transcultural objective base for such ethical commitments as human rights, Rorty wants us to give up thinking that we need to and can establish such justification. Rather, we pledge allegiance to a bundle of human rights because these are the sort of people we want to be—that is, because we are people who do this sort of thing. This grounding of a human rights culture in solidarity rather than in some objective truth does not, he thinks, lead to a pernicious multicultural relativism, but it is, he says, a form of ethnocentrism.

We can well imagine Rorty enjoyed taking a pejorative—ethnocentrism—and turning it into a virtue. Characteristic of his having done so, however, is that Rortian ethnocentrism does not derive out of a simplistic belief in one's cultural superiority. Rorty's version has been rightly dubbed anti-anti-ethnocentrism because it derives from a doubling-back on those who would suppress their Enlightenment values in the face of other cultures who do not share them. He thinks that, while we cannot objectively demonstrate the ontological superiority of the Enlightenment and its talk of human rights, it does have certain practical advantages that deserve to be asserted. Thus, anti-anti-ethnocentrism. We do not need to allow that other cultures that fail to recognize basic rights might well be just as good as ours. An adherence to a concept of human rights, then, is simply the hard-won wisdom of so many horrific stories of suffering emanating from events in which people were treated otherwise—the Nazis' treatment of Jews, the genocide in Rwanda, the Serbian treatment of the Bosnians, the nineteenth-century Caucasian Americans' treatment of the Indians and of Africans, and so on. We don't need to recount these stories and go on to ask: Why is such treatment wrong? Because these stories contain all the answer we will get or need. Rorty's anti-anti-ethnocentrism "scorns efforts by liberals to extend pluralism to include those who do not share their beliefs."[21] and he "urges the abandonment of western liberal anxieties about cultural bias in favour of creative self-affirmation."[22] Rorty will trade-in appeals to transcendent values for those based in the lessons of history anytime.

In the book *Truth and Progress: Philosophical Papers* Rorty expands on the problem of justification:

> most people are simply unable to understand why membership in a biological species is supposed to suffice for membership in a moral

community. This is not because they are insufficiently rational. It is, typically, because they live in a world in which it would just be too risky – indeed would often be insanely dangerous – to let one's sense of moral community to stretch beyond one's family, clan, or tribe.[23]

Rorty's ethnocentrism is the inevitable result of recognizing human finitude combined with the apparent exhaustion of the Enlightenment project of finding transcendence by looking from within the human condition—by generalizing from some aspects of human experience or human being. But that recognition doesn't explain what it consists OF. His ethnocentrism can be roughly translated as "loyalty to bourgeois democracies." He thinks that if we choose wisely, we can have a value system that is admittedly local (because what else is there?) but not relativistic (because locality doesn't preclude the ability to give good reasons).

So, rather than try to find a workaround, what would accrue if we architects simply acknowledged the wisdom embodied in his thinking on this subject? Would it leave us any better off than Zimmerman's anxiety-torn architect? Would it leave us anything to say to Fisher's cultural opportunist? I believe it would. If we are willing to acknowledge an unavoidable ethnocentrism in our values, ethics, and moral codes, then we have the additional burden of both justifying holding those values to ourselves in the face of conflict, as well as justifying to ourselves our continued involvement in moral situations we find to be inimical to them. But what we have gained is that we have relieved ourselves of the obligation of thinking that in doing so, we are engaging in a point of view that is itself ethically dubious. That is to say, we need not feel guilty or apologetic that holding our values when working abroad is a kind of violence against other cultures and that this violence goes against other of our values (specifically, the value of not imposing our unjustified desires on others.) If the client from another culture wishes to know why we hold the values we do, then we can, as Rorty recommends, explain the history which led up to holding and thinking as we do. We know that societies in which bribery is commonplace are poorer than societies in which a concept of impartiality and fairness reigns. We've seen both sides of that coin. We know that societies which disregard environmental consideration pay for it in the long run in a multitude of ways. We've seen it. We don't need to resort to some sort of inchoate, "It's just wrong!" We can give reasons based in historic accounts, if asked. We have seen what happens to architects who become too intimately associated with autocrats and dictators. And we have a good idea what will happen to construction workers involved with our projects in places without workplace safety codes. We have lived the results of the wholesale disregard of our own cultural heritage. We can go along with Rorty here, eschewing appeals to universal rights, the greatest good for the greatest number, and other foundations that, ultimately, prove either too abstract or unconvincing, in favor of stories born out of our history of having preceded other cultures down this road.

What of the concerned Western architect faced with incompatibilities between his or her own pluralistic culture, which has sought for over two hundred years to expand what counts for membership and which prizes the diversity of that membership on the one hand, with a culture which, on the other hand, prizes its purity? There appears little room for middle ground here. Either we proceed from the point of view that enlarging the Enlightenment tent is a good thing, or else we back off in the face of others' demands for cultural purity. Are we imposing our culture's liberal values on another if we refuse to back off? Rorty's quick answer would be "Yes we are," but that we have every justification and need to offer no apology for doing so. Thus, the overly sensitized architect should be able to overcome his hesitation with some degree of renewed confidence. But critics wonder if this isn't too glib an answer. As Abdel-Nour says: "By flattening our complexity, erasing our liberal guilt, denying our voracious appetite for self-deceptive narratives and washing off our self-disgust, (he) chips away at our commitment to other-regard."[24] Abdel-Nour points out that the type of insouciance toward the plight of others exemplified in the Hadid controversy may well find some cover, if not full justification, in Rortian ethnocentrism. "an important practical consequence of the comforts of ethnocentrism that Rorty advocates is that liberals adopting this stand risk normalizing and naturalizing the disregard of others."[25] And just this insouciance seems to be evidenced, as James Riach points out, in Hadid's attitude: "I cannot do anything about it because I have no power to do anything about it. I think it's a problem anywhere in the world. But, as I said, I think there are discrepancies all over the world."[26] Hadid would not be the first architect to discover that self-interest can enjoy much freer rein abroad than in the highly regulated home front. According to Edwin Heathcote: "Part of the attraction of building in undemocratic countries is that they are easy to build for. They commission. They build. They do not let wildlife, local culture, people's houses or the niceties of planning systems get in the way of their vision."[27] Yet this self-interest is all-too-easily cloaked in apparently liberal commitment to respecting cultural diversity. The Enlightenment commitment to other-respect readily transmutes into other-neglect.

But Rorty hangs tough on this issue because the downside of not holding to our moral commitments is too great. He speaks of the bemused Westerner's indecision in the face of cultural difference:

> This bemusement makes us susceptible to the suggestion that the culture of Western liberal democracy is somehow "on a par" with that of the

Vandals and the Ik. So we begin to wonder whether our attempts to get other parts of the world to adopt our culture are different in kind from the efforts of fundamentalist missionaries. If we continue this line of thought too long we become what are sometimes called "wet" liberals. We begin to lose any capacity for moral indignation, any capacity to feel contempt. Our sense of selfhood dissolves. We can no longer feel pride in being bourgeois liberals, in being part of a great tradition, a citizen of no mean culture. We become so open-minded that our brains have fallen out.[28]

Amartya Sen does not seem to think we must give up our commitments either. He says, with regard to the Western Enlightenment concept of human rights, that, "The point to note here is not so much whether we are *permitted* to make cross-boundary scrutiny (a question that is sometimes raised), but that the discipline of critical assessment of moral sentiments *insists* that we have to try to avoid being imprisoned in the parochialism of local perspectives."[29] —thus Sen sees rights talk, not as Western culture putting its imprint on others, but as an entrée into taking a proposed right or rule of action into consideration from multiple perspectives. It seems a little unfair to Rorty to hold with Abdel-Nour that the erasure of liberal guilt is a necessary implication of his ethnocentrism. Certainly, as with the Hadid controversy, it seems a convenient way out. But our sensitized architect need not be rendered less sensitive by his Enlightenment morality. He could find reason to proceed without also having said to himself: "Problem solved!" He could still register the dilemma, and remain poised to revise his views upon further evidence.

For Rorty, rights talk in the face of cultural difference is not only unjustifiable to others, but even worse in his view is that it tends to argue things at a remove from the actual stakes: "The difference between an appeal to end suffering and an appeal to rights is the difference between an appeal to fraternity, to fellow-feeling, to sympathetic concern, and an appeal that exists quite independently from anybody's feelings about anything—something that issues unconditional commands"[30] For Rorty, rights talk is what people fall back on when they have lost faith in the ability to put oneself in others' shoes. Rights becomes an ineffectual stand-in for what is really needed: sympathy and empathy. These things are more likely supplied by literature, and by stories, than by philosophy. We might question whether Rorty has been too eager to dispatch rights talk to the trash bin, for it's hard to see why it commits us to an either/or situation. Can we not make use of *Uncle Tom's Cabin* as well as Kantian moral philosophy to support and bolster one another in the fight against human slavery? Do they not inform one another? If the Kantian categorical imperative is understood as a logical product of enough stories demanding our sympathies, rather than their foundation, then what is the problem with the ineffectiveness of rights talk when dealing with cultures that, as yet, dismiss democracy, impartial justice and the rest of the Western liberal political package? It may be enough that rights talk provides an avenue for generalizing sympathy towards individuals. It is enough that literature and rights talk reinforce one another.

The reason Rorty finds rights talk useless, counterproductive even, is his assertion that culture has its origins in the private realm of subjective experience whereas the public has its origins in interpersonal relations. That is why he thinks that appeal to a public or public good stands little chance of surviving international borders. In what may seem initially paradoxical, the private realm of culture is what we should use to think through cross-national moral dilemmas while the public is the best venue for solving problems within a given polity because when puzzling through dilemmas in cross cultural ethics one cannot count on enough common ground to deliberate publicly—at least with any expectation of change and sometimes, even of personal safety. Therefore one must appeal to stories—to literature—to art, all of which emanate from the private realm of culture and not the public realm of interpersonal relations.

There may be an internal contradiction in the multiculturalists' insistence on the universal validity of multiculturalism; "multicultural universalism." While this contradiction may not mean that regional norms can thereby be dismissed as hopeless, it does suggest more inherent common ground than might first appear between the universalists and the regionalists. It means that what is really on trial is just how much wiggle room can exist between different political norms before one or the other is legitimately seen as beyond the pale—that really, we were already on the same page. The multiculturalists were simply raising some obfuscations. This is certainly how Amartya Sen would see it. Is this true, or is it possible for a culture to simply say, in effect, "this is how we like to do things" without thereby making the larger assertion that everyone, regardless of content, should be able to say the same? "We like to do things this way, your arguments against it haven't convinced us, so we plan to continue as before, but we don't know about anyone else."

Does Rorty give us the philosophical tools to help the overly sensitized practitioner described by Zimmerman get on with his work, while at the same time leaving us any basis for criticizing insouciance? Rorty would have it that we must look beyond the fact of ethnocentrism to its particular content. Our bourgeois, Western, democratic ethnocentrism need not fear accusations of cultural imposition due to its commitment to openness, tolerance and procedural justice. Any value system that sees *those* commitments as impositions on their culture need not overly concern us. Openness, tolerance, and procedural justice are not forms of cultural violence. Thus, Zimmerman's culturally sensitized architect can get on with business. But it doesn't appear that Rorty's ethnocentrism has as much to say to someone all-too-willing to give themselves over to another culture's rules, even when he or she should know better. Architects willing to compromise their values by appealing to multiculturalism are willingly ignoring the simple historical fact that there is no cultural purity within something as large as a polity without substantial oppression. So, while the Chinese or Singapore governments might well present authoritarian rule as a legitimate alternative to raucous democracy, and while they may *claim* to speak for everyone in their polities, Amartya Sen lets us know that they do so without any attempt at securing the legitimate consent of the governed. You can't be said to have truly assented to authoritarian rule without first having had the individual freedom allowing you to well and truly give such assent and this freedom of referendum is something that the authoritarians never willingly allow once in power.[31] Therefore, the apparent widespread cultural consensus is always manufactured. We don't need a transcendent ethic based in human rationality or any other description of what makes humans unique to know this. We shall never be able to step outside a view steeped in the partiality of "we." But the thing that bourgeois liberal morality has going for it is that it is ever willing to be more inclusive. It doesn't depend on the existence of outsiders to thrive. This feature is no small part of its endurance. We have the lessons of history. That is all we have, and that will have to be enough.

The arguments presented in this chapter concerning the profession in capitalism are twofold. First, it is a good thing that the benefits provided by architecture resist subsumption into purely economic goods because in this resistance lies the room for asserting it serves a distinctly public good. Second, in economic globalization the profession finds both the opportunity to extend its reach and learn from others as well as the multiple moral hazards of growing income inequality, the distancing of the public, the creation of international problems resisting solutions at the national level, and relativism. Practicing our profession within globalized capital is unavoidable but there is still room for self-determination in how we do it. Globalization has complicated the concept of the public good but, in some ways, it is also the concept's logical extension—if only we knew what that good is. Before asserting what its good may consist of in Chapter 5, we must first define what the public is and what it is not in Chapters 3 and 4.

Chapter 3

WHO IS THE PUBLIC?

In Chapter 1, I made the two-pronged assertion that the best hope we have for establishing a durable professional architects' ethic is in the public good it serves and that an important reason why the architecture profession has trouble defining the public good it serves lies with mistaken beliefs concerning what the public is. Chapter 2 discussed architecture's deep imbedding within capitalism but went on to make a case for why the public good should not be reduced to an economic good. At the same time, it sought to explain how economic globalization thrusts new ethical challenges at the profession. In both chapters, the importance of subscribing to middle-class, or bourgeois, values was intimated but the conceptual importance of these values has not yet been explained. The task here in Chapter 3 is to begin assembling an ethic of the public good that the architecture profession serves, of which the bourgeois virtues are a constituent element.

The Enlightenment, the Bourgeois Public, and the Architect

The public is clearly an active topic in architecture. On the front table at the American Institute of Architects (AIA) convention bookstore in 2019 the word "public" appeared in no fewer than four titles. *Public Architecture* and *Touchstones of Design: Redefining Public Architecture* by Curtis Fentress and two titles by Jan Gehl—*How to Study Public Life* and *Life Between Buildings: How to Study Public Space*.[1] But, the existence of the public is simply presumed rather than created by architecture and portrayed as more homogenous than it is riven by cross purposes. These mistaken assumptions are fundamental impediments to understanding the public good that architecture may serve.

The concept of the public we have inherited was an invention of the Enlightenment. In the ancient city and into the Middle Ages, even Athens at its most democratic, no concept of a public realm and of personal freedom existed as we know it. In the ancient city, as Numa Denis Fustel de Coulanges puts is: "The state considered the mind and body of every citizen as belonging to it," as a result, there were no limits on the personal invasiveness of the

Figure 3.1 Taksim Square, 2013
Source: Bermanya, Wikimedia Commons, taken June 8, 2013. https://commons.wikimedia.org/wiki/File:June08-GeziParkiTaksimSquare.jpg

ordinances it could pass and enforce.[2] Change was brought about, beginning in the Renaissance, by the rising bourgeoisie: the class of people who most benefitted from the rise of capitalism and who were, therefore, also its most ardent instigators. We can surmise that both the aristocracy and the church, both of which always disdained actually working for money, nevertheless quickly came to depend on the loans and capital infusions only made possible by rapid capital formation by recalling how indebted King Edward III of England became to the Bardi and Peruzzi banking houses of Florence (and which he defaulted on) to get a sense of this intercourse. Even the most regressive European regimes had to take note of the rise in Dutch power engineered by its bourgeois. But capitalism by itself was not enough to force the epic shift to what we know as modernity. Diedre A. McCloskey says that the "modern world was not caused by 'capitalism,' which is ancient and ubiquitous […] The modern world was caused by egalitarian liberalism."[3] Prior to this change in the social order, "the sneer by the aristocrat, the damning by the priest, the envy by the peasant, all directed against trade and profit and the bourgeoisie, conventional in every literature since ancient times, has long sufficed to kill economic growth."[4] Thus began a historic shift in economic power from the church and aristocracy to the bourgeois. According to K. M. MacDonald, "The great change in the shift to modernity was that for the first time since the neolithic revolution the ruling class allowed the holders of economic power freedom of action, and economic power came into its own."[5] For the church and aristocracy this loosening of the leash would prove a fateful mistake from which they would never recover their previous dominance. The great enrichment begun in the Industrial Revolution was enabled by "a bourgeois and rhetorical tsunami around 1700 in the North Sea." With rising economic power came a decreased willingness to submit to the authority of tradition. "Trade-tested betterment" in McCloskey's terms, was a product of a change in the social order, namely, the extension of "a new liberty and dignity for commoners."[6] Bourgeois self-organization, the opposite of elite-managed compulsion, placed the authority of rationality above traditions. As Peter Boettke and Rosolino Candela put it, "The inherited moral intuitions of our small-group cultural past, which laud the warrior-protector or the judicious king, come to be replaced by the rule of law and the bourgeois virtues of ownership, hard work, and commercial innovation."[7]

Increasing recognition that historic rank conferred no superior access to reason or to ability of any kind led to the recognition that people are more or less the same everywhere, only differing by the fortunes of birth status and historic events. This recognition created the situation in which the assertion of human rights emerges, most famously, in the United States Declaration of Independence and its Constitution and in France in the Declaration of the Rights of Man and Citizen. Thus, the collection of ideas we call the Enlightenment coalesced in the second half of the eighteenth century, and its effect was so pronounced that it was even called Enlightenment at the time. For Immanuel Kant, Enlightenment was humanity's casting off its self-imposed childhood: "the inability to use one's own understanding without another's guidance."[8]

For Denis Diderot, the Enlightenment presented a vision of smashed conventions. In *Les Bijoux Indiscrets* Diderot recalls a dream by the protagonist involving a gratifyingly architectural analogy. The protagonist takes flight on a "singular animal" that takes him past a building, suspended as if by magic without foundations, a building devised by old men "lacking weight and strength, and almost all counterfeit" who wear only the scraps of Socrates' tunic. A small boy approaches the edifice. As he approaches, he becomes larger to the point of becoming a colossus by gathering the accumulated experience of Galileo, Pascal and Newton. The advancing colossus carries a torch whose light "penetrated into the bowels of the earth." He strikes the portico of the old edifice, which collapses.[9]

The Enlightenment and the rise of capitalism didn't merely happen to coincide; they were constitutive of one another and mutually reinforcing. Rising incomes were an important proof that the bourgeois ethic was working. The bourgeois era, according to Boettke and Candela, gave rise to "a set of ideas that gave dignity to practices that previously were ridiculed and in many instances despised, and instantiated in the prevailing institutions of the relevant societies, resulted in an alignment of incentives that produced enrichment."[10] Scott Taylor asserts that, "The virtuous practice that a bourgeois ethic can encourage rests on a form of equality, in how we see and talk about each other."[11] This implicit equality allows McCloskey to argue that, not only does it enrich, but is also a source of ethical improvement. It has led not just to vast increases in material well-being but to civility, religious tolerance, cosmopolitanism, and honesty.[12] When Benjamin Franklin wrote in jest that, "Persons of good sense seldom fall into (disputation), except Lawyers, University Men, and Men of all sorts that have been bred in Edinburgh,"[13] he was of course referring with mock dismay to Hume, Smith, and the other men of letters who made up the Scottish Enlightenment. Stewart Sutherland said that, "The disputatious men of Edinburgh to whom (Benjamin) Franklin referred honed their skills in many ways—over a bottle of claret, over the dining tables of the taverns in which they gathered, in many printed papers and books, and in the learned societies that waxed and waned at that time."[14] Thus, the modern public sphere was born. The coffee houses of Britain and the Salons of France became its nurturing venues.

This is the story taken up by German philosopher Jürgen Habermas in his book, *The Structural Transformation of the Public Sphere*, which traces the rise (and decline) of the concept of the public from its Enlightenment origins in the waxing bourgeois class in the eighteenth century as it began to develop its self-awareness and critical potential. The modern bourgeois public has several key identifiers: It is self-organized, open to any person willing to commit to rational discussion (which makes it inherently pro-democracy), and it lies outside of state power. It does not necessarily contain a spatial component but does so fortuitously: it existed in a world of letters as well as public spaces. One of the first formulations of the market externalities provided by public goods came from Adam Smith in *The Wealth of Nations*,

> The role of government had been gradually narrowed until Smith could describe its duties as consisting of only three functions: (1) the provision of national defence; (2) the protection of each member of society from the injustice or oppression of any other; and (3) the erection and maintenance of those public works and public institutions (including

education) that would not repay the expense of any private enterpriser, although they might 'do much more than repay it' to society as a whole.[15]

The modern public bears some resemblance to the ancient Athenian *polis*, but with key differences too. A modern public space, for Charles Taylor, is "a kind of common space [...] in which people who never even meet understand themselves to be engaged in discussion, and capable of reaching a common mind."[16] It is important that the reasons for meeting be held in common, voluntary and mutually understood, instead of merely converging. The collective wisdom of publics, and the sovereign right of the people, means that governments should listen to them and have their actions guided by public opinion. Unlike the bourgeois public, participation in the Greek *polis* was required and nonparticipation was punishable by the state. Furthermore, the *polis*, while self-constituting just like the modern public, was actually the seat of power (such as in its decree to put Socrates to death), whereas the modern public, what we also call "civil society," is independent of the state. "The new public sphere" functions as "a discourse of reason on and to power, rather than by power."[17] This independence is what gives it a critical capacity unknown to the Greeks for, if you are entrenched in your own power, it is impossible to stand fully in criticism of that power. That public action is not in itself an exercise in, nor a preliminary rehearsal in, political power is not a lack, but rather a positive feature of the bourgeois public. This feature allows the public to deliberate, ideally, "disengaged from partisan spirit."[18]

The assertion of the power of rationality when faced with the entrenched interests of church and aristocracy demanding obeisance to their authority is itself ideological. Thus, the modern concept of the public, even though ideally nonpartisan because it is sustained by human rationality, also served as an ideological weapon for the rising bourgeoisie to assert a place of rational discourse against the unearned prerogatives of the aristocracy and the dogmatism of the church. Having finally caught on to the changes it had allowed to accrue, the aristocracy fought back with censorship and banishment (in France) but, ultimately, the match had already been struck. Alexis de Tocqueville's retrospective on these events emphasized that the outsized importance of "literary men" in the French politics of the eighteenth century derived from the vacuum left by the aristocracy that had basically bowed out of politics while the misery of the general populace found solace in the abstractions concerning mutual equality and the rights of men provided by the literary political theorists.[19] This idea chimes with the well-trod assertion that Diderot's and D'Alembert's *Encylopédie ou dictionnaire raisonné des sciences, des arts et des métiers* was the first chapter of the French Revolution—meaning, that the intellectual achievement it represented stood in such stark contrast to the tradition-bound aristocratic society into which it was introduced that it inspired ideas of government similarly freed from hidebound ideas.

As Taylor says, the public sphere eventually became "a central feature of modern society. So much so that, even where it is in fact suppressed or manipulated, it has to be faked. Modern despotic societies have generally felt compelled to go through the motions."[20] This is so because a functioning public sphere does much to self-justify social and political legitimacy.

The rapid expansion and rationalization of knowledge bases combined with the population influx into cities fomented by capitalism created the conditions for the proliferation of learned professions. Macdonald says that, "It is only in modern societies, where knowledge is a unified, autonomous realm and where free markets in goods and services exist, that the opportunity for professions to emerge has occurred."[21] The rapid expansion of cities meant a concomitant expansion of an "extended order" over the medieval "intimate order," and therefore of exchanges between people who do not know each other. The professions are meant to be a partial solution for the problems of trust that arise with these sorts of exchanges.[22] In other words, professions can flourish when the isolation of esoteric knowledge areas meet capitalist free markets in urban contexts.

Architecture, we should admit, was a latecomer to the Enlightenment. The first professional architects' organization in Europe, the RIBA, was not begun until 1834. Although it produced plenty of men of artistic talent in the eighteenth century, its focus remained on the patrons of the past—the church and the aristocracy—and not on the clients of the future. Architecture did not produce any revolutionary intellectual achievement that could measure up to Smith, Hume, Kant, Voltaire, or Rousseau nor to the artistic achievements of Fragonard, David, Watteau and Chardin. While Étienne-Louis Boulée famously proposed that architecture be in homage to great thinkers, he himself contributed no great thought. Though an architectural thinker of some daring, that Claude Nicolas Ledoux is considered one of the intellectual lights of this period only makes it all the sadder. A barrel maker's house in the form of a barrel or phallic-shaped prostitution house? –We could die of embarrassment in the face of Voltaire's and Diderot's intellectual accomplishments. We architects can at least take solace in Jacques-François Blondel, whose *Architecture Francoise* and contributions to the *Encylopédie* did a great service. Not until well into the nineteenth century, and then only tentatively, does architecture catch the Enlightenment spirit with Sir John Soane's thoroughly bourgeois vision of the architecture profession and J. N. L. Durand's scientistic attempt to ground architectural design in a Benthamite utilitarianism (although the results were mostly desultory—a utilitarianism simplemindedly stripped of art). Architecture's retrograde status was in part due to its entrenchment in craft-based production, but also, as stated in Chapter 1, in its tenacious self-identification with aristocratic values. By the time architecture was ready to thoroughly rid itself of its backward elements and enter the vanguard of culture through modernism, it leapfrogged the bourgeois Enlightenment phase of development, going from a crafts-based culture of patronage based in aristocracy and the church, to its Marxist phase (the situation in North America differed from that in Europe—it never occurred to Louis Sullivan and Frank Lloyd Wright to be ashamed of the middle classes). A full-on bourgeois modernism had to wait until the economic miracle decades following World War II on the European Continent and not until Margaret Thatcher came to power in Britain.

An enduring tension within contemporary architectural practice is that while the profession is ineradicably bourgeois, the field's leaders rarely find any source of artistic inspiration in this. Bourgeois is a dismissive term. Habermas recovers modernity's emancipatory potential by showing that the bourgeois class wasn't always the reactionary bastion of conservatism that made it the favorite whipping-boy of avant-garde artists and Marxist revolutionaries. Indeed, even Marx himself respected its achievements:

> The bourgeoisie, historically, has played a most revolutionary part [...] (it) has been the first to show what man's activity can bring about. It has accomplished wonders far surpassing Egyptian pyramids, Roman aqueducts, and Gothic cathedrals; it has conducted expeditions that put in the shade all former Exoduses of nations and crusades [...] The bourgeoisie, by the rapid improvement of all instruments of production, by the immensely facilitated means of communication, draws all, even the most barbarian, nations into civilisation.[23]

You could hardly ask for a better defense of globalization.

Although "the public" was initially an invention to serve the assertions of the bourgeoisie, the logic of their invention outstripped, and continues to outstrip, the boundaries which even its inventors may have envisioned. The same logic by which the bourgeoisie embraced its revolutionary potential to wrestle control over their economic lives also created a market for art and culture. The logic by which a say in government was transferred to all male property owners, the legitimacy of the law was taken from the person of the king, and by which the mutual ownership of public land was established was eventually enlisted beyond the immediate interests of the bourgeoisie to legitimate self-ownership of one's labor, free markets of all kinds, universal suffrage, blind justice, and such public amenities as national parks. Thus was created an unstoppable realm of debate subject to improvement through self-criticism.

This change in power bequeathed to subsequent generations the notion of a public realm that is now taken for granted. This was no small service to humanity, and Habermas is dismayed that in contemporary times, the idea of the public realm is in severe retreat: "Tendencies pointing to the collapse of the public sphere are unmistakable," he notes, "for while its scope is expanding impressively, its function has become progressively insignificant."[24] The very concept of the bourgeois public lay in its openness. "It would have turned into coercion [...] if the public had been forced to close itself off as the ruling class, if it had been forced to abandon the principle of publicity,"[25] thus becoming nothing greater than a new aristocracy. But as long as this principle of openness prevailed, the public realm could be simultaneously both an ideology and something more than an ideology—a gradually realized reality. The public sphere bore the ideology of the end of domination "on no other ground than the compelling insight of a public opinion," that is, the dissolution of domination "into pure reason."[26] Heady stuff! And it is an ideology that still resonates.

Although it is ideological, there is also a fundamental spatiality to the public sphere. For all the talk about the role Facebook played in the democratic struggles of the Arab Spring and in Egypt in particular in February, 2011, ultimately, the most significant moments took place when Egyptians demanded an end to dictatorship by placing their bodies in a significant public space. As Michael E. Gardiner says, "Domination must be resisted first and foremost by bodies," because "power is a material phenomenon."[27] The thrilling events of Tahrir Square (even though they were ultimately reversed) remind us that the function of architecture in the public realm is far from superseded by the digital. The "Occupy Wall Street" movement engaged in the same logic: It did not seek to "occupy" the internet; it sought to critique rising income inequality through the occupation of three-dimensional public space.

Neoliberal Economics, Procedural Democracy, and Utilitarianism

That the public sphere does not fully live up to its ideals is not a valid criticism, Habermas believes, because it always incorporated a procedure for its improvement through rational self-criticism. However, what is a serious problem is the decline of the ideal in modern times as public debate erodes into mere pandering in a process Habermas aptly terms society's "refeudalization." The process of refeudalization begins when competition among elites for public approval is increasingly managed by showy displays of personality; when public space and public goods are increasingly managed by private capital;

Figure 3.2 Tahrir Square, 2011
Source: CC BY 2.0. Image by Ramy Raoof. Army Trucks Surrounding Tahrir Square, Cairo.jpg
https://commons.wikimedia.org/w/index.php?search=tahrir+square+cairo&title=Special:Sea
rch&go=Go&ns0=1&ns6=1&ns12=1&ns14=1&ns100=1&ns106=1&searchToken=ax3iwkoz3
78351zbyqdf7puva#%2Fmedia%2FFile%3AArmy_Trucks_Surronding_Tahrir_Square%2C_
Cairo.jpg changed to greyscale

and where the ideal of participatory democracy has degenerated into "procedural" democracy managed by large bureaucratic institutions.

Adding to these trends is the structural change that occurred in developed nations in which the very idea (certainly the original meaning) of the public realm is rendered nearly incoherent. This has occurred because, as it developed, the bourgeois vision of open participation became progressively clouded in the nineteenth century by the unfair reality of an underclass apparently unable to penetrate into the public realm; a reality that was only overturned by radically democratizing the admission standards. This necessary move entailed the unfortunate side effect that, as it expanded democratically, the public lost its potential for critical self-appraisal and critical opposition to state authority. For Habermas: "The *principle* of the public sphere, that is, critical publicity, seemed to lose its strength in the measure that it expanded as a *sphere* and even undermined the private realm."[28] Habermas's main concern here was the media manipulation of public opinion by the elites, but more recent developments have compounded the negative effects of media manipulation through the creation of captive, bifurcated, and fractured publics that only talk past one another.

The concept of the public realm is further weakened in the effective erosion of the reciprocal distinctions that maintain the boundaries between the two realms of public and private leading to the instability of both. Once the domain of domesticity was largely stripped of its economic function by industrialization, while at the same time its function of socialization was increasingly delegated to outside agencies, the domestic sphere "lost its protective functions along with its economic tasks" preserving "only the illusion of an inner space of intensified privacy." The typical suburb illustrates this trend in vivid architectural terms. "This surreptitious hollowing out of the family's intimate sphere received its architectural expression in the layout of homes and cities." The "disappearance of the salon and of rooms for the reception of visitors in general" in the contemporary middle-class house means not only loss of privacy but also loss "of ensured access to the public sphere."[29] Habermas concludes his account of the erosion of the distinctiveness of public and private with an account of what has arisen in its place:

> The shrinking of the private sphere into the inner areas of a conjugal family largely relieved of function and weakened in authority–the quiet bliss of homeyness—provided only the illusion of a perfectly private personal sphere; for to the extent that private people withdrew from their socially controlled roles as property owners into the purely "personal" ones of their noncommittal use of leisure time, they came directly under the influence of semipublic authorities, without the protection of an institutionally protected domestic domain. Leisure behavior supplies the key to the floodlit privacy of the new inner life. What today, as the domain of leisure, is set off from an occupation sphere that has become increasingly autonomous, has the tendency to take the place of that kind of public sphere in the world of letters that at one time was the point of reference for a subjectivity shaped in the bourgeois family's intimate sphere.[30]

The Covid-19 pandemic has vividly exposed the problems that lay latent in this withering of the productive and public functions once commonplace in domesticity. The perplexing questions of social propriety and the widespread inability to theorize the sudden influx of economic life and the public into the home caused by millions of knowledge workers packing up their offices for their spare bedrooms, pantries, and basements would have caused little disruption in the eighteenth century when the home was also often an economic and public base. What to do about nonintimates suddenly having the ability to peer into one's private realms became the subject of any number of advice columns.

Even if it were possible to reclaim a significant public realm, one capable of critical resistance to power, neoliberal economics would call into question the purpose. According to this view, an intensified private realm of leisure and consumption is the desired end result, so it seems, for which the bourgeois public realm described by Habermas was only a way station. This economic interpretation of the good life has thoroughly inundated other, more politically engaged, conceptions of the good. It has, in particular, hastened the demise of the republican concept of democracy in favor of the liberal interpretation. In a republican democracy, personal initiative and self-improvement serve a greater public aim of participatory self-government that is seen as the essential requirement for and expression of liberty. This republican conception of citizenship has been replaced in capitalist democracies by the procedural, liberal democracy. The liberal democracy operates, instead, on the assumption that the most important prerequisite for liberty is the right to be left alone; the most liberty is therefore secured by government that adopts a neutral framework to the activities of its constituents and lets each decide for himself or herself the ends worth pursuing. "On the liberal conception, by contrast (to the republican conception), liberty is not internally but only incidentally related to self-government. Where liberty consists in the opportunity to pursue my own interests and ends, it may or may not coincide with democratic government."[31] The liberal conception regards the republican view with suspicion; casting doubt on the idea that an engaged electorate can be produced without coercing people to participate and that coercing participation is a peculiar concept of freedom. The republican view is that demanding participation is a small price to pay for the good of true self-government.

While the liberal view seems to abet the withering of the public realm, more aggressively libertarian conceptions even call into question whether such a thing as a "public good" can really exist—echoing Margaret Thatcher's famous assertion that there is no such thing as society: "There are individual men and women, and there are families."[32] The ironically named public choice theory disputes the validity of the distinction between individuals seeking their own gain, and something called the public pursuing a distinctly different set of goods. According to this conception, the public will is not some mysterious, transcendent force for doing good in the world. It is nothing more than the sum of individual actions, and individual actions are primarily motivated by self-seeking ends. Therefore, the idea of serving "the public" interpretation through architecture is just a sentimental fallacy, or else a disguised means of forwarding architects' own agendas. Public choice theory justifies the incursion of the private realm of economic man into the political by arguing that the attainment of something other than the sum of individual goods is not possible; and that the political realm is incapable, therefore, of improving mankind's lot over and above that which can be achieved by the rewards and penalties of the market. For Robert Kuttner, "Logically, if economic man maximizes self-seeking behavior in the economic realm, he also pursues selfish gain in social and political life. But where markets are self-correcting, politics is self-infecting."[33] Politics is self-infecting because it only introduces inefficiencies into market mechanisms; it cannot correct them. If politics is incapable of doing anything but redistributing goods in ultimately self-defeating (because skewed and inefficient) ways, then the associated public realm that makes politics possible is best minimized.

It comes as little surprise, therefore, that as society has become more affluent, the public realm would begin to melt away. The seeds of this decline can be seen from the very beginning: Those who could afford to have always pursued a private conception of the good; the existence of the public realm has served as a sort of consolation for those without the means to create their own worlds. Certainly, the public television show *America's Castles* would support this interpretation. This program inundates viewers with images of houses that not only provided lavish living spaces, but also indoor pools, screening rooms, bowling alleys, and the like. The only reason for public bowling alleys, public choice theory would suggest, is not that people find something unique in bowling in public, but rather the economic limitations of their situations. Robert Putnam's classic compendium, in the book *Bowling Alone: The Collapse and Revival of American Community*, of the many ways in which we are witnessing the demise of civil society since its high point shortly after World War II, confirms this diagnosis. He charts the decline, specifically, of what he calls social capital, but it amounts to much the same thing as a public. The decline and disappearance of business organizations, bridge clubs, political activity, reading groups, and all manner of informal congregating have emaciated the public life. He finds that only two public activities have strengthened since the 1960s: attending sporting events, and evangelical church attendance. (Restaurant attendance has also risen in recent years.) And, he hastens to add, that even sporting event attendance is a rather shabby consumerist substitute for active participation in community activities.[34] Richard Sennett's *The Fall of Public Man* charts the same diminished realm from a different perspective. For Sennett, a public presence was a role one could assume so as to occupy a safe middle ground between threatening strangers and loving intimates. This public distancing enables a civility toward one another that is not possible in our "culture of intimacy," which he finds barbaric. Contemporary trends in housing production would tend to concur. For anyone who can, home has increasingly become a pleasure palace of private amenities. Whether it is the "man cave," the master bathroom spa, or the outdoor living enclave, trends in home design lead to greater isolation and away from engagement. Even in bourgeois homes that still have them, the front rooms of the house are almost never used. The public life is an inconvenient but fortunately minimally demanding activity made necessary by the facts that grocery delivery is hard to come by these days (but maybe not for long!) and having a dry-cleaning plant at home would be noxious.

Well before income inequality began its resurgence, critic Martin Pawley argued that once a public-oriented outlook is gone, it is gone for good: "If the goal system (of commodity-induced nirvana) of Western affluence breaks down, what lies beneath it is not a renewed sense of community through scarcity, but an absolute social collapse without the security of interpersonal and inter-family support [...] Affluence [...] has supplanted all the old systems of mutual obligation."[35] Pawley diagnoses the decline of the public, which he calls community, as something "passionately desired, and consumer goods themselves are valued primarily as tools for social disengagement," and this was in 1973! For Pawley, the word "community" has lost all reality, and its use has become an invocation of fantasy.

To round out the retreat of the public realm, the philosophy of utilitarianism (the go-to moral calculus for assessing cost-benefit analyses) provides an ideal moral justification of the individualistic consumerist and liberal interpretations of the good. Utilitarianism, for Stuart Hampshire, is an outlook which cherishes, above all, "states of feeling as the source of all value in the world."[36] The state of feeling usually identified as most worthy of cultivation is happiness. By privileging happiness as the ultimate good toward which all moral actions aim, utilitarianism provides further justification for the liberal and economic interpretations. This is so because the idea of happiness is virtually unintelligible as a public good. Happiness is something ordinarily experienced by individuals; to have any meaning at all, group happiness is only the sum of individuals' happiness. Utilitarian outlooks favor the idea of architecture as a good that enables certain experiences that increase the overall happiness in the world, and this outlook leads back to the conception of architecture as a consumer good maximized in a society as free as possible from the narrowing, distorting influence of government.

The idea that actions and material goods are ultimately justified by their ability to increase the subjective experience of happiness in the world parallels the hierarchy observed by Joseph Pine and James Gilmore that as capitalism matures and standards of living improve, consumption moves from material goods, to services, to information, and lastly to experiences.[37] This observed hierarchy provides empirical justification to utilitarian claims of the primacy of the experience of happiness, because this appears to be what people really are seeking in the world. Happiness, or the perception of well-being, turns out, after all, to be exactly what people ultimately desire once they have satisfied basic bodily needs. Bentham was right all along about the fundamentals of pleasure and pain. Michael Benedikt argues that architecture, too, has been swept into the justification of design actions through appeals to experience:

> Although rather few architects today are interested in perpetuating the classical-historical pastiche that Postmodernism first favored, many are still interested in the proposition that all buildings—not just amusement parks, museums, hotels, aquaria, and such—ought to provide exciting and memorable encounters, albeit with trendier shards and curves or luminous twisted volumes crammed with electronic paraphernalia. Follow this trend and extend it, and ultimately we must arrive at a new general understanding of architecture—to wit, architecture as experience.[38]

Thus, in the provision and consumption of beneficial experiences, the ultimate good that material items, services, and information all facilitate is finally satisfied by architecture too. These developments lead to the conclusion that, incomplete though the justification of architecture through the principles of classical economics may be, it at least catches the wave of the times in a way that its opposition may not.

The cumulative effect of the logic of classical laissez-faire economics, procedural democracy, and subjective philosophies of the good is to discourage the exploration for new interpretations of facts and values for public benefit. Classical economics instructs that nonintervention in market mechanisms is the speediest route for people to obtain what it is they want; liberal democracy holds that government is incapable of defining the good without coercion; and subjective philosophies of the good intimate that the good can only be found by looking inward. At every turn, the idea that the good can be sought via public forum in rational argument is discouraged or dismissed. Facts are seen as value neutral by these conceptions, and values are seen as incapable of rational exposition (due to their origin in the private realm), and therefore pointless for public debate. Indeed, the very idea of public debate becomes suspicious as being inherently manipulative: "deliberation is taken to be mere logrolling, never legitimate consensus -building or problem-solving."[39]

The Memorial Cul-de-sac

> Only a very small part of architecture belongs to art: the tomb and the monument. Everything else that fulfils a function is to be excluded from the domain of art.
>
> Adolph Loos

Since the memorial, as Loos intimates, has no conventional architectural function, it is unique to architecture as an unencumbered expression of a society's values. Evidence that this trend toward individualism and away from communal conceptions of the good has infiltrated architecture can be seen in the changes that have befallen memorial design since the 1970s.

If we look at an old-school memorial, such as the superb little memorial to fallen firemen built into a grand staircase in Riverside Park in Manhattan, we find that the monument provides a relief bronze of a horse-drawn fire engine heading to a fire flanked by sculptures representing Duty and Sacrifice. A fountain, suggestive of the means with which fires are extinguished, completes the composition. An inscription on the east side reads:

Figure 3.3 New York Firemen's Memorial, 1913. Harold Magonigle, architect
Source: Tom Spector

> To the men of the fire department
> of the city of New York
> who died at the call of duty
> soldiers in a war that never ends
> this memorial is dedicated
> by the people of a grateful city

Simple, graceful and suffused with the noble purpose for which the firefighters gave their lives, there is no suggestion that the fallen need be individually named. It is enough that firefighters as a group are recognized for their heroism. This sort of corporate recognition, unless the memorialized were of the stature of a Lincoln or a Jefferson, combined with storytelling images and comforting words, was the order of the day until 1982 when the Vietnam Veterans Memorial by Maya Lin opened. Here, architectural minimalism in execution is paired with a fastidious naming of over 58,000 United States service members killed or still MIA in the war to profound effect. Minimalism, and an emphasis on the individual lives cut short by the war coupled with a refusal to in any way congregate those involved into the service of something greater has become the mainstream for memorial design ever since. Both the Oklahoma City National Memorial and the New York-area 9/11 memorials do much the same thing. The names of the individuals lost are encased in a minimalist architectural environment thought to be suitably somber to meet the occasion. The Holocaust Memorial (memorial to the murdered Jews of Europe, 2005, Peter Eisenman, architect) in Berlin takes things a step further. Since the magnitude of death was too great to list individuals, a field of 2,711 enigmatic concrete stelae is installed as a surrogate or proxy for the incomprehensible number killed.

Certainly, part of the rationale behind this trend toward minimalism combined with individual naming is the change in purpose or occasion for the more recent memorials. They exist to remember the victims. In any event, what is not suggested in these memorials, what is never suggested, is that these people constituted a community driven by a common purpose, or that they made a mutual sacrifice for some greater good. Furthermore, the architectural minimalism, in which figuration is eschewed, and in which there can be no words of comfort, no images provided, no stories told, while being justified as a means toward achieving something more profound than would be possible with the expression of mere conventions, deliberately circumvents the possibility of the comfort of community, of having committed to something greater than the individual, and in fact give visitors little reason to return because it gives them so little to do.

In Oklahoma City, and again at the World Trade Center, a hastily erected fence around the bombing site became coopted by a grieving city as a makeshift altar to which mementos could be affixed. Through grief a public was born. The chain link gave mourners a way to participate through trinkets and stuffed animals left there, as well as a means to communicate with each other over time and therefore a reason to return. While these spontaneous memorials were eventually banished from the national memorial sites, in Oklahoma City a 210-foot long segment was retained just outside the Western side of the memorial, even though it was not seen as compatible with the design intent of the memorial proper. Though spontaneous participation has declined considerably in the ensuing years, the chain link fence is the one place where grieving and memory can be renewed, refreshed, and displayed for others. The 9/11 memorials have no such mechanism. Nothing prevents people from leaving flowers or other memorabilia, but they are regularly removed as detractions from the purity of the memorial itself. The Berlin memorial's refusal of all conventional narrative content leads to a complete lack of any prescriptive suggestion on the proper way to use it. Kids play hide-and-seek, couples meet for picnics on the stela, others wander around a while wondering what it is all for, and they are all equally correct or equally incorrect in how they use the place.

Thus, we have entered a cul-de-sac in memorial design. It was not always the case, but today individualism rules the day in this most expressive and pure type of architectural work. Since the congregate public with which to engage is reduced to grieving individuals, the sum of whose grief is no greater than the sum of the individuals' grief, the loss no greater than the sum of the individual losses, and a sense of common purpose nowhere in evidence, there is no need for conventional symbols or words of comfort we might share. All communication operates at the preverbal, therefore preconventional, level of subjectively experienced grief engineered by minimalism. A museum off to the side, while always a welcome repository for the exhibition of related artifacts is no substitute for the memorial. You can't divide a memorial into a grief exhibit and an educational wing with the same impact as when they are incorporated into a unified expression. There is no need for something we might cooperatively contribute to or maintain. There is nothing to do but take a photo, consume the spectacle and leave, except on designated anniversary occasions. The public is only allowed spectator or consumer status, because there is no greater entity proposed with which we might all take part. Lives were lost. There is no greater good. No looking forward. Full stop.

Figure 3.4 Vietnam Veterans' Memorial, 1982. Maya Lin, architect
Source: Tom Spector

The Manager, the Rich Aesthete and the Therapist

These three sources of justification for individualism: neoliberal economics, procedural democracy, and subjective philosophies of the good align well with philosopher Alasdair MacIntyre's contention that society is increasingly fractured into three character types, the manager (justified by the needs of procedural liberal bureaucracy), the rich aesthete (justified by laissez faire economics), and the therapist (justified by the quest for happiness).[40] What is important to note about these roles, MacIntyre insists is that in their fulfillment no one is held responsible for helping to achieve the good in the overall sense. The rich aesthete follows his or her own proclivities with impunity, the manager is responsible only for facilitating the achievement of previously approved ends, and the therapist, also conceiving of the ends as given is only responsible for helping turn "maladjusted individuals into well-adjusted ones."[41] These roles or character types have specific restrictions placed on their moral options. To be a character is to merge your individual traits with a social role.

The manager or managerial outlook is devoted to economically and efficiently matching whatever means are available to previously set ends.

WHO IS THE PUBLIC? 73

Figure 3.5 Oklahoma City National Memorial and Museum, 2000. Butzer Design Partnership) (210 feet of the fence remain outside the memorial)
Source: The Walking Photographer, March 18,2018. CC Share-Alike 4.0. changed to greyscale. https://commons.wikimedia.org/wiki/File:Oklahoma_City_Bombing_7.jpg

Therefore, the manager's performance is measured by effectiveness at implementation. The ends are given in advance and the manager is responsible for implementation toward those ends. The managerial outlook and role obliterate the distinction between manipulative and nonmanipulative social relations. Why is this? Because concern over nonmanipulation is addressed somewhere else by someone else, perhaps in the political arena, but the important point is it is not addressed by management.

This loss of an ethical role in society in favor of a managerial one leads to the existence of the second character type, the one we are all supposed to aspire to: The Rich Aesthete. The rich aesthete is the paradigm consumer; someone who has complete leisure to seek the best the world has to offer. He or she restlessly seeks goods on which to shower his or her means. Good for the rich aesthete means enjoyment of what life has to offer. Hedonism rules. By "Good" is meant "Good for Me." Our economic system is predicated on the desirability of getting to be one of the people who occupy this niche and the restlessly consuming rich aesthete is the economy's prime mover. When economic data points downward, encourage the consumer to spend more. As with the manager, the rich aesthete is not charged with seeking the good in the

Figure 3.6 National 9/11 Memorial and Museum–2011. Michael Arad, architect; Peter Walker, landscape architect; and Daniel Libeskind, master plan
Source: Tom Spector

overall either, but only the good for the individual. The manager makes sure the goods are available; the rich aesthete makes sure there is a demand for them. They are both serving the same cause and neither is required to have a care for the greater good.

The third character dominating modern life, MacIntyre tells us is that of The Therapist. The Therapist is not allowed to weigh the desirability of various ends either. Rather, the therapist is charged with turning maladjusted individuals into adjusted ones, of turning neurotic symptoms into directed energy. What the therapist does not do is engage in moral debate regarding the desirability of the things one must adjust to (they are reified); nor the desirability of the character under treatment. The search for truth is displaced by psychological effectiveness. The world is not held accountable and neither is the patient. The project is just a matter of fit. Evaluating whether or not the world into which you are going might well be crazy is not part of the therapist's remit.

Now, we could dispute that MacIntyre's list is exhaustive, but that is not the point. The point is that if MacIntyre is on to something, then no one in

Figure 3.7 Empty Sky Memorial, New Jersey, 2011. Frederic Schwartz and Jessica Jamroz, Frederic Schwartz Architects
Source: Tom Spector

our culture today has the responsibility for seeing to it that the ends that are given, short of the exceedingly narrow ends afforded by hedonism, are, in fact, worthwhile, or good ends according to the widest possible interpretation of the good. Everything runs on autopilot, the invisible hand of capitalism, or the great conspiracy of capitalism, (depending on your politics) or, perhaps, the debased values of a degraded and faded Judeo-Christian ethic, or the great chaos of our pluralistic society. But no one is discussing the good in the widest sense. Everyone is partisan and this includes our politicians, our professionals, and our public intellectuals (if indeed there are any of those left). Even the idea of citizenship is horribly debased from its nineteenth-century conception. Our culture cultivates conflict between political parties or opposing factions as a sort of compensation for a lack of an ethic. The underlying theory being that at least if conflict between local conceptions of the good is allowed to be expressed, we can be sure that everyone has had his say and that coercion is kept to a minimum. MacIntyre's diagnosis helps explain why it can be so difficult to get a discussion of the public good off the ground these days. We have plenty of values … Everyone has their values. There are managerial values, aesthetic values, therapeutic values … just no ethics, at least not in the sense of taking responsibility for subscribing to a comprehensive interpretation of the good.

Now, it is interesting to consider the practice of architecture in relation to these three character types. Is the architect a manager, an aesthete, or a therapist? We could well make a case for the role of architect taking important dimensions from all three character-types, but yet still without feeling charged with the task of somehow fusing them to help to establish important ends. Certainly the architect is a facilitator: "So, you want a 12,000 SF house with his and hers hot tubs? Sure, I can make that happen." We would not necessarily consider it part of our role to question the client's desires and whether his-and-her hot tubs were actually desirable and necessary. But, of course, the architect also, if only often as surrogate, occupies the role of the rich aesthete. We cultivate aesthetic experience to a highly refined degree. An architect who is not aesthetically motivated is almost certainly a bad architect. The fact that we rarely have the money to indulge our tastes only seems to serve to make them felt all the more urgently. But the classes of the rich aesthetes are often our reference groups, their tastes are our tastes, and we seek to help them further their pleasurable consumption of the world by providing one of the most expensive and prestige-enhancing consumer items of all.

If we spend a great deal of our professional careers helping the rich consume more pleasurably, at the same time we often operate on the level of therapist for the masses, those affected by architecture but not rich enough to actually commission and consume it. We help people adjust to their surroundings by manipulating the environment just enough, cosmetically as it were, to keep it from actively repulsing people, to aid in the project of keeping people docile, and by scripting the use of buildings sufficiently so that they rarely call attention to themselves or rub people the wrong way. We oil the built environment enough to keep down its clanks and groans so that people will continue to toil away in it—because, after all, would it be kind to exacerbate things for the purpose of irritating people?—just enough to keep all the capitalist machinery running, and give them the prospect, if not the general reality, of becoming rich aesthetes themselves someday.

This grim description, of the role of architect spread across all three characters but neither integrating nor questioning them, does however, hold the seeds of opportunity, because even if none of these roles holds the obvious key to becoming a lover of wisdom, a seeker of truth, or dare we say, an architect in its full normative sense, it at least provides a source of inner conflict that may lead us to start making these connections; to start considering the good in the broad sense again. We can start making sure that opportunities for self-organizing activities are made available in our work so that the public impulse, when it does crop up, can be accommodated—at least that our buildings and places we create don't fight it.

Despite its early rhetoric of being for the people, modernism never really embraced this notion of allowing self-organizing activities to blossom. The characteristic modernist dwelling is a totalizing environment with little yield to alternative conceptions of living. This dominating characteristic of modernism was recognized early on. Adolph Loos satirized modernism's tendency to totalizing design when he told the story of the poor little rich man whose architect-designed house was so perfect that he couldn't move or add a thing or even leave his slippers lying around else the aesthetic would be destroyed.

The manager, the therapist, and the rich aesthete may be the dominant character roles as MacIntyre says, but architects can use their role-spanning power to envision new ways to engage the public with a moral vision of suitable breadth.

Publics and Counterpublics

Thus, the concept of the public inherited from the Enlightenment is fractured and much reduced but it is not completely done in. A variety of vital forms of opposition to the architecture of consumerism can be found to exist still. The cumulative effect of the opposition is the realization that the pursuit of private goods in the built environment affects others in ethically significant ways, that economic interpretations of the good in architecture underserve important areas of human affairs, that the value-neutral presumptions of procedural democracy often serve to stifle expressions of valuing as much as they serve to allow their unfettered pursuit, and that conflicts of values are capable of patient, rational, exposition. In the face of the declining fortunes of the bourgeois concept of the public, these movements often take the form of what Michael Warner describes as a "counterpublic." Counterpublics "are defined by their tension with a larger public. Their participants are marked off from persons or citizens in general […] A counterpublic, against the background of the public sphere, enables a horizon of opinion and exchange; its exchanges remain distinct from authority and can have a critical relation to power."[42] In other words, they function much like the original bourgeois conception of the public described by Habermas— before that conception became so inclusive as to lose its critical capabilities. The chief difference between counterpublics and bourgeois publics is that counterpublics do not necessarily take responsibility for promoting all-encompassing visions of the good. Counterpublics are born out of repression, unlike the bourgeois public which was born out of a rising sense of autonomy. The counterpublic opposition movements Warner identifies seek to change opinion within the larger public as much if not more than they are concerned to pose a critical opposition to state authority—the traditional role of the bourgeois public. As the concept of the public at large is increasingly ground down, these counterpublics offer the best chance for meaningful change. Further, multiple counterpublics may coexist and mutually reinforce each other. Thus the idea of multiple publics is born even as the Enlightenment bourgeois public is reduced. This helps to explain why opposition movements such as Gay Pride and Black Lives Matter continue to flourish while the general architectural public is hard to identify. Architecture's counterpublics are its most viable options for critical engagement with power.

The reasons behind the assertion made in Chapter 1, that thinking of the public as "everyone" or as adequately represented by the state is woefully inadequate, are perfectly illustrated by the Black Lives Matter movement which emerged in 2013 following the shooting death of Trayvon Martin in Florida, gained momentum in 2014 when Michael Brown was shot by police in Ferguson, Missouri, and resurged even more forcefully in 2020 in the wake of the deaths of George Floyd in Minneapolis and Breonna Taylor in Louisville, also at the hands of the police. Black Lives Matter is best understood as a counterpublic because it speaks *to* the general public but does not assume it speaks *for* it even while it employs the structural features of the bourgeois public. It is self-organized and uses rights language, but maintains a critical distance from the larger public's complicity with institutional racism while simultaneously opposing the state. If the architecture profession wants to do its part to overturn institutional racism, it will need to respond to the pointed criticisms expressed within Black Lives Matter and Black Visions rather than the more watered-down versions that eventually emerge from the larger public. Architects of good will wishing to participate in solutions to the injustices addressed by components of the Movement for Black Lives, such as housing insecurity and the carceral state, may do well to start these efforts at home, with improving access to the profession and representation within it by people of color. An important place to start is with the leadership provided by the National Organization of Minority Architects (NOMA) in the United States, whose mission, retooled in 2020, is to "foster justice and equity in communities of color through outreach, community advocacy, professional

Figure 3.8 Trafalgar Square, Pride March, 2010
Source: Tom Spector

development and design excellence."[43] Among its initiatives are the summer camps provided by Project Pipeline, which seek to address the lack of racial diversity in the profession by interesting young people of color to enroll in architecture school. Noisily supporting such initiatives as Project Pipeline and public-oriented organizations as NOMA are tangible ways the profession can show its sincere commitment to the public good in place of the vague platitudes of health, safety and welfare.

However, building the pipeline into architecture school is only where the task starts. Once in school, students of color will find that their instructional histories and exemplars are Eurocentric and white. Their access to informal networks of potential employers for summer work experiences are often less extensive than their white counterparts at the same time that often coming from households of limited means results in high levels of student loans accumulated upon graduation.

Beyond addressing the challenges of school, the profession must first recognize and then seek to improve the fact that increases in racial diversity and inclusiveness within firms has budged little in recent decades. One could host a party for every black woman architect in the United States in a modest-sized

Figure 3.9 Black Lives Matter, Charlotte, NC

meeting hall.⁴⁴ It's not surprising that many black architects report, in addition to all the other stresses of being an architect, the feelings of isolation within the firms they work at the same time they experience the self-consciousness of representing their firm's diversity.⁴⁵ The partnership between NOMA and the Large Firm Roundtable (LFRT) in the United States is a welcome development in this regard. To further the cause of diversity in the workplace, Michael Marshall suggests that standards for diversity within firms could be improved by "an institutional rating system or certifications for architectural firms that will establish what are good standards for achieving diversity and inclusion,"⁴⁶ inspired by the LEED certification system for buildings. Such a system would provide the twinned benefits of simultaneously publicizing innovations in diversity while encouraging firms to greater achievement.

As they move up in the profession and consider starting their own firms, successful careers for practitioners of color are often inhibited by the lack of boardroom access to decision makers that is also a legacy of institutional racism. While it is neither a good nor a bad feature of the profession that the decision to hire an architect is often the result of building individual relationships of trust between architects and their clients, our culture's institutionalized racism inhibits the very opportunities to develop such relationships between black architects and the moneyed, largely white, clientele to begin with. This inherited situation often leads architects of color feeling relegated to competing for "set-asides" at the margins of conventional practice. Making efforts toward casting-off the rewards system of its patronage orientation will help the profession defeat the racism constraining its ability to show what serving the public means in practice.

A different, but equally powerful perspective on the limitations of Habermas's public realm is contributed by feminism. For Nancy Fraser, it is possible for a postmodern conception of the public sphere to succeed if it acknowledges that participation requires a parity which has historically been hard to come by and must be worked towards, if multiple publics exist in the face of persistent inequality, and if the domains of public and private are allowed to be contested. The importance of contesting the domains, and therefore the boundaries, of the public and private realms lies precisely in the fact that the relegation of the problems of, for instance, child care to the realm of privacy has the effect of denying a role for ethics; of isolating, say, spousal abuse from public scrutiny has the effect of making it invisible; and when examining a public problem like inequality in the workforce of overlooking its origin in the home. Fraser doesn't believe that the pathologies that result from distinguishing between public and private are insurmountable, but in order to be overcome they must be contested. The feminist perspective on the ethics of public and private has much to contribute to the discussion of improving the public realm. This is where we turn next.

Chapter 4

PUBLIC AND PRIVATE

Perhaps the most striking example (of a counterpublic) is the late-twentieth century U.S. feminist subaltern counterpublic, with its variegated array of journals, bookstores, publishing companies, film and video distribution networks, lecture series, research centers, academic programs, conferences, conventions, festivals, and local meeting places. In this public sphere, feminist women have invented new terms for describing social reality, including "sexism," "the double shift," "sexual harassment," and "marital, date and acquaintance rape."[1]

As Nancy Fraser's quote asserts, the feminist counterpublic is paradigmatic of a well-functioning modern public realm. But even more important than as an exemplar, feminism and in particular, feminist ethics, has done more than any other subdiscipline to explore the boundary between the public and the private, a sense of which is needed for the task of reconstructing a guiding vision of the public good of architecture that can clearly demarcate both the realm it encompasses and the area outside its ken.

A major criticism by feminist moral philosophy of traditional male-dominated discourse has been its predilection for making unwarranted and self-serving assumptions regarding what is legitimately "private," and outside the purview of moral philosophy, and what is "public" and therefore open to philosophic scrutiny. The boundary between the two spheres should be regarded as more fluid than it has been, feminists argue, because, if anything has been learned from feminist inquiry, it is this: that the home is politically charged and the agora is populated by those who rely on the caring relationships of the home.[2] The idea that the walls of domesticity mark an abrupt boundary between public and private and between the moral and the beyond-moral is portrayed as nothing more than a convenient fiction for those who want to dominate women at home and exclude them and the lessons of domestic life from their moral theory.

Figure 4.1 Isaiah Davenport House, Savannah, Georgia
Source: Tom Spector

These architectural ideas imbedded in feminist moral theory are intriguing metaphors for philosophers, but for architects they also suggest at least the potential for being perceived as having actual influence on the built environment. Thus, when philosopher Virginia Held argues, for example, that "the claim that the family is particularistic while the polis deals with what is universal is questionable even in terms of existing institutions. And if the wall between the private and the public were dismantled in the ways many feminists advocate, support for the claim might erode,"[3] architects will tend to want to explore this dismantling literally. Such literalism could hardly be misplaced; architecture is too important a participant (as well as a symptom) in the creation of the very possibility of making distinctions between the public and private domains to be considered a mere afterthought. The domains of public and private, hearth and agora, do not just happen in an open, undifferentiated space: they only occur in carefully devised settings. With this inherent spatiality in mind, it is more than plausible to maintain that architecture lies just below the surface of any discussion of feminist ethics and that architects can do much to either challenge or reinforce stereotype-reproducing boundaries. However, making a normative case for the rightful location of those boundaries has caused considerable dissention within feminism. The 2020 pandemic experience has brought with it fresh questions for feminist ethics to consider in this regard as boundaries between public and private are suddenly shifted when the public invades the home with Zoom conferences and staying in-place becomes a matter of public health.

The Dilemmas of Feminist Ethics

Feminist ethics' initial impetus came from Carol Gilligan's *In a Different Voice*, which sought to extract a distinct ethic of care derived from women's experiences as caregivers in the home. Challenges to this concept quickly emerged when it became clear that a distinctly feminist ethic faces a dilemma regarding the emphasis that should be placed on constructing a radically feminist-derived philosophy from the ground-up versus a more conservative renovation of philosophy's traditional discourse. Margaret Urban Walker sums up the dilemma in architectural terms. She questions "whether maternal paradigms, nurturant responsiveness, and a bent toward responsibility for others' needs aren't our oppressive history, not our liberating future; whether 'women's morality' isn't a familiar ghetto rather than a liberated space."[4] Joan Tronto puts the dilemma in historical perspective: "The notion that women occupy the private world, which has qualities that protect and preserve morality from a public onslaught"[5] is an artifact of the global changes of the eighteenth century as the world became less parochial and more cosmopolitan. This was a world in which women were largely excluded. Therefore, a distinctly feminist "ethic of care," derived from interactions with people you are intimate with in the home proposed as a feminist answer to the masculinist "justice ethic" derived from interactions with strangers in the public realm, only helps to reinforce, rather than redefine, its boundaries. Carole Gilligan, the first person to articulate the ethic of care, has repeatedly insisted that the different voice she discerned when listening to women's reflections on their moral predicaments is a complement to, and not a substitute for, the traditional emphasis that moral philosophy places on justice reasoning.

Others are not inclined to regard the situation as conservatively as does Gilligan. Believing that the tradition of Enlightenment-inspired moral philosophy systematically puts women in a subsidiary position, some critics insist on rejecting "its values and concerns" completely.[6] Either Gilligan's caring perspective must be so radicalized as to become a thoroughgoing repudiation of that tradition, as Joan Tronto advocates, or else the caring orientation must be regarded as only a foundation upon which to elaborate an altogether new conception of ethics, as Nel Noddings and Annette Baier do. Either tactic turns out to be problematic, however, because the first "underestimates the discursive power of philosophy" itself, while the second "overestimates [...] its claims to universality and neutrality."[7] Thus, feminist philosophers of a more radical stripe than Gilligan find themselves in something of a bind too. Trying to reject or radicalize traditional moral philosophy will probably not work because of its "discursive power" to constrain how philosophy can even be thought about, while trying to join the traditional discussion is likely to fail because that discussion's very concept of neutrality is ideologically loaded, stacking the deck against those who question it.

Other philosophers think this lose-lose scenario needlessly defeatist. Traditional moral philosophy has its historical prejudices, but those who seek to employ the caring perspective to renovate this tradition do not think them as pernicious. They think of feminism not as a final stage but more instrumentally as an intellectual ladder to be eventually thrown away once the goal is reached.

At stake is the question of whether moral lessons and concerns derived from characteristic experiences of family and private life lend themselves to systematic development in moral argument, and whether taking these lessons out of their characteristic environment among intimates and into the necessarily less personal environment of public life allows a more nurturing overall moral environment to develop, or whether it instead makes a mockery of those lessons by setting them up in a situation in which they cannot possibly succeed. This persistent dilemma of feminist moral philosophy stands to be informed by the collective vision of feminist architects.

The Agora and the Hearth

The environments in which male-dominated, justice-oriented moral philosophy arises on the one hand, and those in which feminist awareness of a different set of values dominates on the other are neither interchangeable nor disembodied. The exact opposite is the case. The justice perspective serves the needs of those who assert their autonomy in the traditional agora of public life among other similarly autonomous individuals. A prime need of such people is to establish the rules of behavior for mutual advantage among those who might otherwise feel little to no ties or responsibility toward each other. Hence, contractarian conceptions of moral behavior, where rights and responsibilities are explicitly spelled out and agreed to, gain plausibility. This situation differs markedly from the one that women characteristically experience as caregivers in a family setting. The prime need here is to be attentive to the specific needs of intimate others, and to foster the same attitude in others, in a setting of interdependence, mutual affection, and interest. Rather than being made explicit, rights and responsibilities in this setting can appear completely open-ended. An inherent inequality between these two settings presents itself. For Tronto, "as many feminists have noted, the division of public and private life is not a case of separate but equal spheres. Indeed, the public is of considerably more importance than the private, and since political life is identified with public life, the relegation of caring to private life means that it is beyond (or beneath) political concern,"[8] this, despite the fact that the private sphere can be infinitely more demanding on the moral agent.

Determining to breach the walls that help sustain this inequality is one thing, but deciding just how to bring the values of one sphere into the other is another matter. Although successes and failures in one setting necessarily affect the other, it appears, at first blush at least, that the differences outweigh the similarities between the two, and that therefore relatively little transference from the values of the agora to those of the hearth is likely. This leaves as an open question how effectively the caring perspective can perform in public life. By actually giving substance to the boundaries that create and separate public and private, architecture stands to help philosophy envision the plausibility and desirability of bringing caring into the agora, or justice into the home. By creatively addressing these boundaries and settings, architects might do something more substantial still: they might actually help transcend the discussion's current limitations.

Here are some questions that span both architecture and morality: How plausible and desirable is it for the workplace to be a more caring environment? What would such a workplace look like? At a time when work for many has rapidly moved back into the home, has this shift been accompanied by any compensating shifts in moral boundaries? When the boundaries between public and private are substantially breached as they have been for many due to the 2020 pandemic, does this in effect remap the home as a more public realm? Will the pandemic experience of substantial work from home remap public and private boundaries at the office?

A central function of architecture has traditionally been to create beautiful boundaries. Has this been such a bad thing? Has beauty been used to paper over abuse and domination? Or is it, instead, that beautiful boundaries are the very stuff of the good life? Certainly, architecture has had a love affair with walls: domicile enclosures, privacy fences, neighborhood boundaries, city walls; all serve moral ends by allowing the close coexistence of activities that otherwise do not normally mix well for the ultimate benefit of enhancing individual lives and allowing the development of more complex communities. All this has not been without its hazards, however, as architecture professor Beatriz Colomina notes poetically: "Public space is produced by a violent effacement of the private […] The interior is the steel wire of the cannon. It is the very substance of the weapon. The interior is therefore precisely the possibility of the violence that becomes visible outside it."[9] And Colomina is right: when most mass shootings in the United States begin with an incident of domestic violence the "domestic" side of the phrase seems inadequate, "'intimate partner violence' or 'intimate partner terrorism'[…] is a bit more like it."[10] Where is the boundary between public and private in such circumstances?

Even if it seems heavy-handed to insist that these walls all come down, Joan Tronto points out that a dilemma over how to proceed persists:

> There is a danger if we think of caring as making the public realm into an enlarged family. Family is a necessarily private and parochial understanding of caring. The only way that transforming the political realm into "one big happy family" can work is to import with that notion some ideas that seem inherent in family life: hierarchy, unity, partiality, that are anathema to a liberal, democratic society.[11]

Perhaps architecture can join this discussion by reconsidering the layers of enclosure that modulate the distinctions between public and private space, public and private behaviors, public and private values, and what you see within the scope of the Zoom window, and thereby open the discussion up to new possibilities.

The Performance of Care

The problem of introducing the caring perspective into both mainstream moral theory and the built environment may be more radical than this. To make caring a serious contender in the agora, it will have to be politicized and recast from a description of a sentiment and orientation to something operationalized and described in functional terms, in much the same way that contractualist theory is presented. This is the possibility Joan Tronto sets out to explore, and the results are intriguing for architecture. Tronto analyzes care as a process involving four components: (1) identifying a need; (2) taking responsibility for it and "determining how to respond to it"; (3) actually performing the meeting of the need; and (4) recognizing that "the object of care will respond to the care it receives." Redescribed in this way, caring can be generalized enough to go beyond consideration of intimates, even to caring for the environment. "Care is perhaps best thought of as a practice," in opposition to the "sentimentalized and romanticized" idea that caring is about an outlook, a disposition, and a personal relationship.[12] Tronto notes the similarities between her vision of caring and consequentialism (the view that what ultimately matters is the best outcome, however that may be defined), and indeed, in the way she has outlined it, caring becomes indistinguishable from consequentialism. "What is definitive about care," she writes, "seems to be a perspective of taking the other's needs as the starting point for what must be done."[13] Tronto notes that under this redefinition, care can absorb a much broader outlook: "We suggest that caring be viewed as a species activity that includes everything that we do to maintain, continue, and repair our 'world' so that we can live in it as well as possible. That world includes our bodies, our selves, and our environment, all of which we seek to interweave in a complex, life-sustaining web."[14]

At least one author from the architectural side of the fence would agree with this. Brenda Vale's essay "Gender and an Architecture of Environmental Responsibility" aligns a feminist orientation in the built environment with an environment-friendly outlook that closely resembles caring. Vale sees the traditional role of women as being one of standard-bearers — the guardians of incrementalism and piecemeal action and as role models for achieving an architecture of greater environmental sustainability. She proposes that the conservative role women occupy in general is more likely to be environment-friendly than would a more radical one. She argues: "An architecture that is environmentally responsible has to belong to its locality; it has to work with the elemental forces that surround it; it has to be self-effacing."[15] It is no stretch to characterize these virtues as caring ones. Vale further believes that the traditionally described women's role leads to an experiential approach to learning, which in turn leads to an environmentally responsible architecture by involving users in processes as well as in goals.

Care, in Tronto's schema, still excludes some activities: "the pursuit of pleasure, creative activity, production, destruction. To play, to fulfill a desire, to market a new product, or *to create a work of art*, is not care."[16] Thus, architectural programming, which takes the other's needs as a starting point, would appear to fit within this performative concept of care, while the aesthetic-creative act of architectural design would not. This is a dismaying turn. Feminist architects, and architects in general, would probably want to use the process of architecture-creation to express ways of caring about others and about the built environment too. Indeed, this seems like fertile territory for architectural exploration rather than an area to avoid. Perhaps Tronto simply got caught up in an unintended boundary here—equating the creative, artistic act with self-expression and self-assertion, rather than recognizing the many orientations of creative activity and of art. Her exclusion of the creative act of architecture from a performative conception of caring is telling, however, of the general perception both within and outside architecture that the best designers are concerned with such presumably masculine pursuits as formal perfection and aesthetic ingenuity, and that for such designers connecting people in caring ways with their environment is merely a consolation. This attitude toward lionizing artistic autonomy finds its complementary opponent in traditional moral philosophy, in which artistic matters are considered to be of lesser consequence than moral concerns.[17] Perhaps we need go no further to understand why star-design architecture has characteristically taken the caring perspective to be as much a weakness as a strength: the disdain is mutual.

A feminist approach to architecture seeks to overcome the long-dominant idea that an overly solicitous outlook is a weakness, and that "catering to needs" is death to a serious pursuit of form. Feminist architects seek to divert the tremendous value architecture has long placed on the pursuit of form by emphasizing instead the central purpose of creatively reaching out to others through both the act of designing, if not making, buildings and of restructuring the profession of architecture as a collaborative rather than heroic discipline. But feminist architecture struggles with the same question as do feminist ethicists on this point: Can a feminist approach to architecture be satisfied with remodeling or must it completely rebuild architecture's traditional values? One of the most visible ways the problem has been approached in recent years is by recontextualizing it into the more general topic of the "construction" of gender itself.

Gender Boundaries

Feminist philosophers worry that accepting the domestic derivation of a distinctly different ethical voice only reinforces accepted paternalistic boundaries. As Nancy Fraser argues, the terms "public" and "private" "are not simply straightforward designations of societal spheres: they are cultural classifications with rhetorical labels. In political discourse, they are powerful terms that are frequently deployed to delegitimate some interests, views and topics and to valorize others."[18] More radical is the proposition that gender itself is constructed and that it has heretofore been fashioned primarily to serve the interests of heterosexual men. If this is true, then the unquestioned embrace of a care ethic may be a refusal to creatively explore the more interesting boundaries of what it means "to be a woman." It is not coincidental then, that in places where gender identity is most freely trespassed and reconstructed, such as in San Francisco, so are the boundaries of public and private. In San Francisco, trespasses over traditional boundaries of public and private originate in both the public and private domains. Areas of life formerly considered private—such as the conceiving and raising of children and even the care of one's pets—are now opened up to civic legislation and intense public scrutiny, while other areas of life formerly enacted in the most private circumstances, such as the practice of one's sexuality, have become commonplace in the public sphere. Here, the erosion of public and private boundaries is a direct result of gender exploration, of questioning what constitutes appropriate sexual or nurturing behavior, by whom, where, and when.

Architecture stands to help people explore these issues (or hinder them) by making environments that are relatively conducive (or inhibiting) to exploring the interplay of public and private. How might a feminist approach give a different "voice" to such explorations?

The answer may prove elusive. It must be recognized that, so far at least, attempts to determine the impact of gender explorations on architecture or of architecture on gender explorations have not convincingly shown much influence running either way. While reinterpreting the boundary of public and private through the reconstruction of gender norms continues to be creatively interpreted by people of all walks of life, architecture has been a clumsy tool with which to give expression to gender and sexuality. It appears that the needs posed by the reinterpretation of gender norms are simply not all that different from other kinds of human needs to which architecture already responds.

For example, George Chauncey explicitly refutes the idea of "gendered space" in great detail.[19] In his study of homosexual appropriation of the built environment in New York, almost everything depends on social constraints and homosexuals' creative responses to those constraints. Architecture, in his account, is at best a prop but oftentimes simply incidental to the narrative. It appears ideologically neutral. The notion that the built environment is gendered and sexualized all too often seems less determined by the physical features of the space than by the motives and outlooks of those who want to use it in a certain way. The notion of gendered space can be broadened, however, as it is in Aaron Betsky's book *Queer Space: Architecture and Same Sex Desire*, by the assertion that architectural space can be "queered" through actively resisting its oppressive normative features. But Betsky's notion ultimately appears able to include any architectural acts offered in the spirit of opposition. Resisting the norms of gender ends up having relatively little impact on the specifics.[20]

In a more concrete example, the Lesbian-Gay-Bisexual-Transgender Community Center in San Francisco, "the world's first building built from the ground up by gay money, political influence, and organizational strength" is ultimately disarming in its conventionality, despite some strong symbolic gestures, such as the entry choice it presents between an "exposed" glass Market Street facade and a "sheltered," stucco-covered side entrance (which to many contemporary visitors may appear as a puzzling anachronism) as well as other moments where the subject of visibility is distilled, according to Jacob Ward.[21] While it reportedly serves its constituency well, and is planning an expansion, its several floors of offices, meeting rooms, and multifunctioning spaces can easily be imagined to serve any number of other uses. This could hardly be a failing of the building: explorations of gender and gender-related issues simply don't appear to be particularly form-generating in comparison to such constraints as climate, technology, physical comfort, and cultural expectations, or more to the point for this discussion, the constraints of public and private as they are currently experienced. It may just be that we have more in common

Figure 4.2 San Francisco Lesbian-Gay-Bisexual-Transgender Community Center
Source: Dreamyshade - Own work, CC BY-SA 4.0, https://commons.wikimedia.org/w/index.php?curid=60352660

as human beings than we have in differences resulting from sexual or gender expression when it comes to what we need from our architecture and what our architecture can be reliably said to express about those needs.

The same could be said for the Center for Women's Studies and Gender Research at the University of Florida, by Kim Tanzer and Caroline Constant, which sought to instantiate several principles of feminist design in its form and spatial organization.[22] Informal gathering spaces, room arrangements that sought to discourage the formation of hierarchies, and a unique "knot garden" at the entrance were some of these design elements. But what one comes away with from the authors' recounting of the story of this facility is that it is hard to put one's finger on what exactly makes this an example of feminist design instead of more generally a progressive design. Once again it seems that architecture is simply not good at expressing gender-specific ideas.

The refashioning of the "women's voice" question into "the construction of gender" question at least in what has presented itself so far gives us little help in reinterpreting public and private more creatively and appears to do nothing to relieve the dilemma of whether a feminist ethics must raze or build upon traditional values to perform adequately. If anything, these examples suggest that it doesn't much matter, architecturally speaking, which side of the dilemma feminist architects eventually opt for. The architecture itself will still be more conventional than not, no matter how radical the reconstruction of gender identity. Therefore, a blanket rejection of traditional architectural values is likely to achieve little. The dilemma, I suggest, is better resolved in a piecemeal fashion, through the actual consideration of unique design issues, and through consideration of the voiced needs of those who stand to benefit or suffer from a specific architects' design decisions. A more radical and general stance does not appear to be any more likely to be an effective catalyst for change.

Exploring the Boundary between Public and Private in Contemporary Practice

Nancy Fraser's insistence that counterpublics be empowered to address other, larger publics, to confront them with evidence of destructive bias for received assumptions regarding what belongs in the public realm and what in the private, was precisely what was at stake in the revelations of workplace sexual harassment in architectural practices in 2018 when one of architecture's most celebrated practitioners was called out as a serial sexual predator early that year. In quick order, an architectural counterpublic was born; one determined to confront architecture's larger public with the actions by men that were formerly kept out of sight in the private realm. This successful counterpublic came after failed previous attempts to crack open the private world of architectural employment, such as by the website Insidearch.org, which were always shut down by the concerted efforts of powerful architecture firms. The anonymous creator of "Shitty Architecture Men" was moved to create and circulate a spreadsheet of complaints about incidents of harassment because of a culture where "Many firms are structured around a 'Great Man' with a singular vision, which lowly employees are tasked with carrying out. It's very top-down. This can create power imbalances that make junior employees vulnerable to exploitation, whether it's harassment, pay inequality, or something else."[23] Pressure was brought on the American Institute of Architecture (AIA) emanating from the organization's New York chapter (the effort was led by prominent New York architect Frances Halsband) to make public a more definite stand than it was heretofore willing to do. The successful pressure resulted in an amendment to the AIA Code of Ethics in October of 2018 to include the provision that:

> Members shall not engage in harassment or discrimination in their professional activities on the basis of race, religion, national origin, age, disability, caregiver status, gender, gender identity, or sexual orientation (Rule 1.401).

And along with this rule, the equally long-overdue provision that:

> Members should provide their associates and employees with a fair and equitable working environment, compensate them fairly, and facilitate their professional development (Ethical Standard 5.1).[24]

Gender pay equity is a problem on both sides of the Atlantic. In Great Britain, it is estimated that women architects earn 25 percent less on average than their male counterparts."[25] While in the United States, the Bureau of Labor Statistics estimated in 2014 that "among full-time architects, men earn on average 20 percent more than women."[26] Should the profession in the United States be heartened because the organization made a definitive statement, or embarrassed that this didn't occur until 2018? By allowing an entirely different voice to be heard, one that makes a caring perspective foundational to design decisions and professional practice, a uniquely feminist interpretation of architecture just might improve the situation for everyone.

These issues were not unknown to the profession even prior to 2018. Even though women fill nearly half the slots of architecture schools and constitute a fast-growing percentage of practitioners "a disproportionate number of women leave architectural practice."[27] The takeaway findings from a study in the United Kingdom in 2003 could find no single reason for women defecting from the profession. Rather, survey respondents cited a long list of reasons, including a culture that was not family friendly, stressful working conditions, a macho culture, sexism, and paternalism that amount to a steady drip, drip, drip effect, an almost daily clash of values, that made continuing on in the profession so unattractive. Thus, women architects (who may or may not be feminist architects) must grapple with the same dilemma facing feminist philosophers: Is it good enough to simply occupy "a place at the table" formerly belonging to men, or does the situation call for a complete departure from existing patterns of practice? It should be noted that the first woman to shatter the pinnacle of architectural practice by winning the Pritzker Prize, Zaha Hadid, did so through a body of work that completely emulates the mold of the autocratic, uncompromising form-giver attributed to masculine ideals. Either by temperament or by pragmatics, Hadid did what it took to win in a man's game. If there is a distinctly women's voice in architecture, she was not interested in exploring it.

The women who left the profession did not cite as a reason to exit that they did not like making architecture. Overall, they wished they could have stayed. What a debacle for all concerned! The women who leave lose their chosen career, their firms lose good employees, and the profession loses some of its best and brightest. Now, we have reason to believe that, as more women enter and persevere in the profession, values and working conditions are being adjusted. Certainly, we can see that what was formerly kept private is getting a public airing. But just how much and how quickly the boundaries are redrawn between the private business of firm management and the public good of fair treatment across the board we will likely only know in retrospect, as we see how many vulnerable employees continue and prosper.

Moral and Artistic Values in the Evaluation of Architecture

In the wake of accusations of serial sexual harassment, the question whether we are still "allowed" to like the architecture of Richard Meier in light of such revelations was inevitable. This is a strange question on its face.[28] Its strangeness stems not only from the presumed overlap between a creator's behavior and his artistic production on the one hand, but also from the strange word "allowed." Who or what is doing the allowing or disallowing? Try to name an art form not riddled with creators of bad, very bad behavior. Presumably, someone asking such a question is wanting to know if they can "allow" themselves to enjoy a positive aesthetic response to, say, the Getty Museum & Institute when they have a good idea that the creator of this ensemble was harassing female employees at the time of its creation. And, if they do "allow" themselves to sneak some enjoyment of something that they have a good idea was partly created in an atmosphere of harassment, then are they guilty of being callous? There are many sides to this question and much of it depends on a willingness to transgress traditional boundaries of public and private. The very ubiquity of doleful behavior on the part of many of architecture's most well-known creators would seem to make it impossible, according to such standards, to like anything. It seems these infractions are as ubiquitous as speeding on the interstate, and so, the very ubiquity tends to insulate both its perpetrators as well as us from taking exception to individual acts. "It's all compromised, so it's hopeless to get worked up" is the natural outgrowth of such recognition.

This question also touches on one's aesthetic philosophy. If I am willing to regard the Getty, untroubled by moral qualms, as an artistic masterpiece, then does that make me a formalist ready to jettison all contextual matters (the working conditions under which it was constructed, the regime it was designed to legitimate, the people unfairly displaced, and so on) when engaged in questions of artistic judgment? This implied subscription to formalism, then, might serve as a reason I should not "allow" myself to enjoy the building without reserve. Aaron Betsky would have it that, "In an ideal world, we should be able to separate the work from the man or woman who made it, but in the real world, the cult of the 'genius maker' so thoroughly defines the way in which any art is made and received that we cannot ignore questions of character when we look."[29] Placing aside, for the moment, what would make the formalist world more ideal than a contextualist world (judgment would be simplified, but does that improve it?), one presumes he must be referring to the regrets stemming from a loss of innocence, but his answer to the perplexity posed by the Meier scandal is to lay what he implies must ultimately be a reduced estimation of the work at the feet of the cult of the genius maker which doesn't ALLOW us to regard the work, as apparently in the ideal world we want to do, in isolation of questions of sexual misconduct.

With these prefatory remarks in hand, I propose that the single question of what we are allowed to like needs to fork into two different questions that are more nuanced and tractable. On the one hand is the culture within which the behavior of an abusive creator is not only tolerated but even respected up to a point, as something of a perk as well as characteristic of such people who flout the status quo in their lives so that they can become artistic innovators. "As in life, so in art?" How is a Frank Lloyd Wright supposed to reign in his sexual appetites without calming his creative spirit? There is no definitive answer to this question. No statistical analysis of great creators will tell us if we can separate an artist's treatment of other people from his or her creative force. Some creators will insist that it's all part and parcel—the work and the personal; that the search for freedom and innovation cannot be tamed and that, therefore, there can be no drawing of a public-private boundary in such lives. While others can subscribe themselves to middle-class, instead of aristocratic values, in their treatment of others, at least in their work lives, if not so closely in their personal lives. But this lack of definitive answer does not at all translate to the lack of a right on the part of those of us affected by and bound up with this culture of production to condemn it and demand change. If we find the aristocratic values of the few so abusive to the many that the risk of taming the creative impulse is worth the potential cost, then that is our prerogative. But, our right and ability to demand that entitled aristocratic attitudes be quashed does not provide any direct paths to regarding the work itself as relatively less meritorious. To make some progress on the question of whether we can "allow" ourselves to like Meier's buildings now that we see him as a serial sexual predator, we will need to look at the second fork of the question: What, if any, connections can be made between works and their creators' morality? As is so often the case, the issue can be clarified if we look at a blatant case—let's consider the racist architecture in the Old South.

Racism figures prominently in art forms emanating from the South and its effect on the artwork can take a number of directions. It figures prominently as subject matter in narrative art forms such as in literature and in movies: in *Huckleberry Finn*, *The Color Purple*, *To Kill a Mockingbird*, *Gone with the Wind* or more recently, *The Help*, and *Go Set a Watchman*, in which racism both sets the context for dramatic conflict and sets events in motion. In general, the degree to which these works express an appropriately condemnatory attitude toward the institutionalized racism of the South improves their aesthetic quality. Scarlet O'Hara's total self-absorbed disregard of her black servants' plight within the context of the civil war and its aftermath creates disjunction for many contemporary readers with the heroine, even though the book succeeds in its goal of portraying a completely self-absorbed character. This disjunction was once again news in 2020, when the movie was pulled from televised presentation in order to be properly prefaced for its difficult moral vision. This recognition of a relation between judgments of aesthetic merit and appropriate moral attitudes fits into the shock and confusion that many readers experienced in the release of *Mockingbird's* sequel, *Go Set a Watchman*, in which *Mockingbird's* racism-fighting protagonist is revealed as himself racist.

The operations of racism in works of literature are illustrative of the more general topic of the relationship of art to morality. Much of the discussion of the interaction between art and morality centers on the role that an artwork's moral vision may have on our evaluation of its artistic achievement. Opinions on this matter range from Clive Bell's complete autonomism—in which art is seen to be both completely independent of morality as well as superior to it, to Berys Gaut's moralism which asserts a direct correspondence between a work's moral vision and its artistic merit. Other possible positions on this matter include Noël Carroll's formulation of moderate moralism, and Eileen John's opportunistic moralism—both of which assert a looser, but still discernible, connection between an artwork's moral vision and its artistic merit and Daniel Jacobson's antitheoretical position that it is impossible to actually take a position on this matter because all points of view apply at one time or another.

An interesting and moderately fruitful discussion has emerged, but one which has been singularly unhelpful when it comes to evaluating difficult works of architecture. It has been unhelpful because, on the one hand architecture, as one of the paradigmatic nonnarrative arts, is often treated dismissively. It has also been unhelpful because, on the other hand, it fails to recognize architecture's very real, if unwitting, agency in acts of moral depravity.

The autonomists, the moderates, the opportunists and the antitheoreticals all want to line up against the moralists to ask such questions as: If, as the moralists insist, there is a directional relationship between art and morality, then why do we not reject the callously murderous actions of Macbeth and of Hamlet as lowering those works' aesthetic quality due to the unacceptability of Shakespeare's moral vision of nonchalance toward treating characters as mere collateral damage? Daniel Jacobson, Noel Carroll, and Arnold Isenberg have all discussed these particular examples. Although both Macbeth and

Hamlet, who seem all too willing to send characters off to their deaths, clearly have large moral failings which go unremarked, the plays are none the worse for their protagonist's moral failings. So the conclusion must be that morality and art do not run strictly together. So true—as far as it goes. But I would not be the first to observe that, not surprisingly, at least part of the answer to this charge is that the fact that Macbeth, Hamlet and their victims were all fictional, should count for something in this discussion. It should figure prominently into the distinctions we make when considering the relationship between morality and various art forms. Architecture, on the other hand, does not create works of fiction. Every built work of architecture, by the very nature of the art form, is real. Discussion of the relation of art to morality largely ignores this crucial fact. So, if works of architecture can be implicated in real, not fictional, actions and outcomes, then their agency is of an entirely different order. Most art forms are innocuous in this sense, and hence a discussion of their moral failings is fairly trivial. Not a one of those novels or plays can actually, physically hurt you, and let's be equal opportunity here and throw painting, music, theatre, and sculpture into that category as well. The difference between fictionalized moral depravity and real moral depravity is that one is … real. A work of architecture, Scarlet's home Tara, features prominently in both the story and the racism it embodies, and it would have been, with little doubt, built on the backbreaking labor of enslaved persons. But Tara is a fictional work of architecture, not an actual work of architecture, and so we can bracket its unpleasant backstory just as we can go along with Hamlet's treatment of Rosencrantz and Guildenstern for the sake of Shakespeare's plot. But what are we to think of all the real Taras out there?

Antebellum, Greek Revival, *Gone with the Wind* mansions still exist by the thousands across the South. Though the Greek Revival originated in Britain as an antiquarian movement following the documentation and dissemination of Athenian architecture in Britain, the style was transported first to the northeastern United States where it was seen as emblematic of participatory democracy before it landed in the South as the very image of a slave-holding society.

When we encounter these still extant works of architecture we may feel initially torn.

For on the one hand, it makes no sense, as Clive Bell would no doubt agree, to scold a building for the actions of its owners, much less a style of building, especially a style that has obviously been seen and used in so many different ways. The Greek Revival's cooption into the slave-owning power structure of the Old South was not its doing, nor was it predictable. Attributing morality to inanimate objects is usually a fool's errand.

On the other hand, there is reason to also feel strongly that there is something distasteful about being invited to appreciate a grand Greek Revival Antebellum mansion purely formalistically—ignoring the violence that was once perpetrated in it, around it, and in its very making. It's understandable if an African American family visiting one of these houses on a home tour is less than enamored. And though the Greek Revival's role in creating the very image of this racist society was not its own doing, we have to admit that, once here, it performed its role quite ably. In other words, its characteristic formal elements—peristyle colonnades, pediments, and all the rest—helped create an image legitimating inescapable violent power mixed with cultural dominance.

So how do we reconcile these competing conclusions? IS there any reconciling them?

While works of architecture are poor story tellers, they are quite revealing of a society's values. There is no such thing as accidental art absent a significant bundle of human intentions. Immaterial elements—ideals, goals, artistic interests and the like, do certainly go into the creation of an artwork, so why would we be forbidden, in the appreciation and evaluation of that artwork, from accessing the immaterial, sticking only to the formal elements that present themselves? The Greek Revival in the slaveholding South was the IDEAL artistic vehicle for helping shore-up the illegitimate power structure of the time. It cloaked the inherent violence of the regime in trappings of cultured elegance. In its peristyle forms, it helped reinforce an image of an inescapably panoptic control by the slave holder, and the gleaming image and sturdy proportions spoke of the regime's resilience. These formal features of the Greek Revival were not at all incidental elements in its appeal at the time. So now, when we visit these formally beautiful structures for their place in history as the central imagery of the Old South, or for the ingenious artistry involved in solving such compositional problems as making use of the deep architrave required for a formally successful rendition of the style, or resolving the stocky proportions of Doric columns at a residential scale, we are bracketing those elements of their existence that we find unpleasant or inconvenient or conveniently irrelevant today. But when it comes down to it, not until Naziism and Stalinism came along could we find works of architecture in modern times so thoroughly implicated in the noxious political aspirations of a regime as we can with the Greek Revival of the Old South.

If we disallow even a mild formalist assumption that we can distinguish between artwork and context—that to say "this is the artwork, and that is the context" we smuggle in a value judgment that presupposes the outcome. So, no matter all the moral considerations they are willing to place on an artwork, the artwork is still understood as having an independent existence. The work is the work and context is context. But this position seems to assume the exact thing that we want to question: What is context and what is artwork? Only strict formalists are consistent on this issue. The content of a Greek Revival mansion is the assemblage of wood and bricks and paint. Everything else you decide to allow in as relevant to an aesthetic judgment is going to have its arbitrary and inconsistent moments. But to allow this, is to already give in to the racists because then they have gotten us to bracket their artworks. To even say that we know that a work is its formal elements + its moral vision is to still allow its formal elements a partially independent existence. That is why it is necessary to assert that racism is a constituent feature of the artworks we know as Southern Greek Revival architecture. It is not their unpleasant context. In this instance, at least, either aesthetic judgment can include racism, or else racism is capable of an aesthetic component. The Greek Revival mansions of the antebellum United States have no such independent existence. With the antebellum Greek Revival mansions, you are in effect leaving some cards on the table if you don't insist that their ability to facilitate racist intentions ARE a measure of their success. The better they are formally, the worse they are morally because their formal successes make the illicit slaveholding regime look all the more culturally legitimate. With novels and films, the works' moral vision may well be integral to the work, but in every case their moral impact is external. It's their potentially pernicious effect on people's attitudes and future actions that generates moral concern—think of Marquis de Sade's fiction, for example, or the movie *Triumph of the Will*—but the artwork itself does not do these things. Our moral qualms revolve around what actions and attitudes judging the artwork to be successful might lead to. If the stage directions for the play *Hamlet* called for actually murdering actors in its production for the sake of realism we would have second thoughts about it. But in the same way that we can assert that cars are dangerous or guns are dangerous, buildings are dangerous. Works of architecture, because they are real and not innocuous, actually can be enlisted to do some of the work of their masters. They can intimidate a subjected population directly as a result of their successes in formal terms. With these considerations in mind, I think we are considerably past the ability to discount the problems emanating from the moral vision that goes into creating works of architecture. First of all, they hold the potential for real agency. The Greek Revival mansions of the antebellum South helped sustain a violent regime through their formal beauty, material way of being, and their associations with other, legitimated, cultures. Second of all, they can be quite revealing of people's intentions, and hence, in this admittedly truncated way, they do tell stories.

History is quite filled with oppressive and murderous regimes making architecture. Does this argument require us to, for example, have to look differently on the Egyptian pyramids? We know, or should know, that the construction of these magnificent architectural objects was on the backs of the immense suffering of the conscripted populace, and that an important function of them was to assert the unending and total power of the pharaohs. But we are justified in feeling considerably less tugged on by that knowledge than by the knowledge of the truth of the antebellum mansions because that culture and that civilization is not ours and it no longer exists. While that culture left some impressive architecture, it does not still reverberate in our social dimension. Therefore it's ok to let it go, and simply react to them formally. Moral philosophy recognizes that humans feel differently about the here-and-now than they do the distant and past. This is part of our human makeup which utilitarians have found it a stubborn thing to try to dislodge. It takes a lot, in other words, to make us feel the call of a famine 5000 miles away as strongly as it does the hungry among us. The first generations of Germans after the Nazis felt the guilt and shame of World War II very strongly, but each subsequent generation is less affected, and rightfully so.

While there certainly is *some* distance between us, here, now and the slaveholding antebellum South, linkages are altogether too easy to trace, making it feel inappropriate to drop contextual considerations for a strictly formalist interpretation, or retain but sanitize out the unpleasant aspects of the contextual. And I think this is why it may still be important and appropriate to include moral concerns in our appreciation of these formally beautiful structures. There was a time I wanted to give them a pass: "Yes they are beautiful but …" but am no longer willing to discuss them as artworks marred by a flawed moral vision. It was that moral vision that created them. They are suffused with it. There is no distancing ourselves from it. Maybe, hopefully, someday time will sanitize them as it has for the pyramids. But not here, not now.

With these thoughts in mind, we may now be in a better position to take up the second fork of the question regarding architects with distinct moral failings. The question of whether those moral failings should factor into our appreciation of the work can be answered with more assurance if we look into and come to some determination about whether those moral failings manifest themselves in some constitutive way in the work. Do the formal elements of the work facilitate, condone or promote sexual harassment? Are they directly coercive? If you can answer yes to that question, then you have found good reason to lower your estimate of its artistic accomplishment. But if the answer is less direct, let's say that their artistic success facilitated the creator's career to go on and do more harassing while in business, but that nothing in the artwork helps to do the harassing, then we may also want to be correspondingly hesitant to decry the work. The question of rescinding awards to such creators is similarly vexed. It is all but impossible to tease out the work from the creator when giving a retrospective career award. Is it possible to separate, say, an AIA 25-year award to a building from a Pritzker award to an architect and assert that one is not to the architect while the other is? If only our culture wasn't so conditioned to credit only an individual creator and willing to anonymize the many other talented people who brought the project into fruition, this question wouldn't be so intractable. If one member of a team is personally discredited, even if it's the star player, we have good reason for that fact not to bring discredit to the whole team. Such situations give further reason to work on the culture which facilitates the rise of abusive stars because good people suffer, and that is enough to know.

To add to further consideration of this evaluation problem, any art form will have its expressive strengths and weaknesses. Architecture is well-equipped to express ideas of power and dominance but appears to be a clumsy vessel for the expression of sexual attitudes. Despite a few instances, where we see, for example, a Doric column as masculine and an Ionic column as more feminine, or certain tall buildings as phallic, there appears to be little in the arrangement of building materials or spaces that is inherently sexual or, as discussed earlier, gendered. Therefore, it would make sense that some creators' moral failings would be more easily teased out of their architecture than would others. Architecture has many tools at hand to express the desire to dominate others in a generalized sense, but not to pick out certain groups for dominance unless other social arrangements facilitate such access. It has tools to express the desire for anonymous surveillance of others and tools to express aristocratic status, and to repel outsiders, but even the harem at the Topkapi Palace in Istanbul has nothing distinctly sexual emanating from its forms and materials. Attempts to demonstrate the existence of "queer space" showed that same sex desire reflected in architecture is entirely based in malleable conventions of use and can exist anywhere. Thus, to say we "see" sexual harassment in a building is to reduce the give-and-take between artwork and observer to only "give." That is, to project thoughts and feelings about the creator on to a building but to fudge the question of where, exactly, or what motifs in the building work to reinforce this kind of depravity. While ineradicable negative subject response to a building might be unavoidable for the victims of a creator's harassment, and while I have argued that distinctions between context and work have a normative component from inception, that assertion does not go so far as to erase the physical reality of the work into full subjectivity. Recognizing that the work has some sort of independent existence, even if the exact limits of that independence are up for discussion, places some responsibility on the person exercising judgment to point to the actual features within the building or artwork doing the action claimed of it. An inability to determine such features should caution those seeking to make

Figure 4.3 Green-Meldrim House, Savannah
Source: Tom Spector

long-term determinations of a building's artistic merit based on the actions of its architect.

The Caring Perspective in Practice

Unfortunately, the caring perspective has yet to become a strong theme of feminist writing on architecture. The themes most often encountered instead are: (1) exposing peculiar or even somewhat shocking instances of women in history influencing or responding to the built environment;[30] (2) second generation-style feminist critiques uncovering the "masculinist" uses of the built environment to dominate women;[31] and (3) critiques of contemporary theory.[32] Only rarely do essays such as Jennifer Bloomer's "The Matter of the Cutting Edge" surface to confront the boundary between the agora and the home by contrasting (in this case) the caring perspective of women watching children playing in the yard with the academic's critical eye trained on women at the cutting edge of cultural progress. Reflecting on the provocative comment by Camille Paglia that, left in women's hands, civilization would still be in grass huts, Bloomer observes that "the grass hut stands in for anything undeveloped, unadvanced, not extruding itself along the exalted line of progress," thus hopelessly associating the domestic sphere with stasis.[33] Bloomer's essay suggests that a resolved integration of the caring and justice perspectives is just not in the offing. Instead, a reasonably complete human life will continually attempt to balance unresolved and competing elements of both, thus, the architectural need for boundaries, walls, and separations: to allow each to have a domain in which it can receive full expression. The same suggestion arises from the few essays by women practitioners reflecting on their own design experiences.[34]

Lori A. Brown's discussion of the architectural implications of the abortion debate in the United States reflects on the latent oppression in the public-private boundary: for those in power, the boundary is fine when they want women to stay in place but inconvenient when it obstructs their political agendas, such as with abortion clinics. As Brown says,

> Abortion and domestic violence occur in the most private of space, the space of a woman's body. However, both intersect with the public when debated, legislated and accessed. This inversion of something so personal and private being debated within the realm of the public is a strange and troubling paradox. In the sense that through the making of *publicness* the issues around each are ultimately manipulated into something no longer about women's bodies.[35]

Brown and others, suspicious of inherited binaries such as public/private, suggest that we should theorize a "third space" that triangulates with the public and private realms as a place of gathering where transgressive acts can be enacted. What this sort of space would consist of architecturally is hard to envision, and whether it could be counted on to provide a haven for the oppressed is doubtful. Certainly, the discussion of queer space would indicate a lack of any objectively architectural characteristics of such spaces when these things tend to dissolve into pure subjectivity. While its promoters would have it that third space is a way the oppressed undermine oppression, it would seem that restrictive country clubs, masonic halls, conspiracy-theory web sites and Klan meetings equally qualify as places where transgressive acts of exclusion can be safely enacted.[36] The name itself suggests a hazy lack of specificity.

The importance of exploring the caring/justice boundary in contemporary architecture makes it disappointing that explicitly feminist writing on architecture has not been particularly interested in finding or discussing instances where women have creatively explored that boundary.[37] A prominent instance of caring women wielding considerable influence in the built environment comes from my home state of Georgia. There must be many others.

Anna Colquitt Hunter (1892–1985) sparked a group of seven women into action in 1955 in a successful attempt to save the historic Isaiah Davenport House in Savannah—less than 24 hours before its appointment with the wrecking ball. What began as a "crisis-oriented preservation group" transformed, through raising the money for an innovative revolving fund, into a "civic organization committed to planned revitalization of the entire urban area."[38] Having now directly saved over 350 historic structures and indirectly sparked the rehabilitation of over 1000, it is no overstatement to assert that an entire city was saved by the caring of a group of women who came to be known as the Historic Savannah Foundation. Their outrage at the fast-disappearing historic fabric of downtown Savannah to impersonal and (as it turned out) shortsighted economic interests was turned into a pioneering program of saving, rehabilitating, and returning to self-sufficiency hundreds of threatened eighteenth- and nineteenth-century buildings. These women, who were heretofore not of activist temperament, nevertheless became one of the most potent political forces in the community, not by favor-trading and intimidation, but by being willing to take substantial personal risk to protect the objects of their affections. These women denied the impersonal forces of the agora, and instead employed the caring perspective as a successful foil. Their achievement in fashioning what became the largest historic district in the nation eventually achieved world fame.

The women of Historic Savannah found the ability to forge ahead and negotiate the difficulties they faced by treating the objects of their affections as one would treat family and loved ones. To do so they were willing to take tremendous personal risks—with their finances, their health, and their reputations—but were conspicuously unwilling to allow those risks to be imposed on the built environment they sought to preserve. Their attitudes were conservative in the sense of keeping the ideas of conserving and nurturing uppermost, and entirely progressive otherwise. Aesthetic risk held little interest. The women of Savannah made nurturing the historic environment back to self-sufficiency as much a priority as the initial act of creation. With Historic Savannah, the quest for self-sufficiency required creating a critical mass of restored and functioning structures so that the entire movement in Savannah would develop a momentum independent of the relatively small amount available at any one time from the revolving fund. Finding the grit and determination to ensure that the objects of one's affections thrive even after one's passing represents the caring perspective at its best. Anna Colquitt Hunter and her friends' actions demonstrate that caring need not be a "familiar ghetto" but instead may be a source of strength, creativity, and beauty. The women of Savannah triumphed in the public sphere by holding firmly onto values forged in the private. Clearly, the world could use more of this, not less.

The suggestion to emerge is that the familiar boundaries of public and private, caring and justice, hearth and agora, are not, at least, inherently the tools of oppression. They have certainly been used that way, but they have also been used to good purpose. The caring perspective, nurtured in the private domain, can achieve spectacular success in the agora with enough determination, but is ambiguous on the advantages of a distinctly delineated public domain. Is the agora a necessary precondition for the development of the values of the hearth, or its impediment? Furthermore, the boundary between public and private does not remain firmly drawn but shifts according to a culture's needs at any given time, as we have seen during the Covid-19 pandemic. This disputatious boundary between public and private has done much to call attention to what is at stake, however, when we attempt to erase it. An architecture profession committed to serving the public good must be willing to question, rather than assume, the boundaries between public and private it may subsequently play a role in reinforcing or dismantling.

Chapter 5

TOWARD AN ARCHITECTURE OF PUBLICNESS

Architecture as Infrastructure

The largely pro bono or in some way subsidized design practices by such entities as the San Francisco-based Public Architecture, the now-defunct Architecture for Humanity, and the many individual initiatives by architecture firms around the world who do good works and generate considerable publicity for doing so have begun to provide proven creative outlets for architects' public spirit. The work of these entities regard serving the public good much as lawyers do it: as something that must be achieved outside the boundaries of for-profit practice. However well-meaning and welcome it may be, the shortcoming of this approach is that it marginalizes the pursuit of the public good as merely an ameliorative use of the profession's excess capital. It's wonderful if you can do it, but if you can't, that's OK too. If we want to be able to make the stronger assertion that the architecture profession's limited market protections are necessary to enable its crucial role in advancing the public good, then we need a conception of the public good of architecture for which this outcome accrues as a *direct result of everyday architectural practice* and not as something done on the side, when we want to, and as a gratuity. If we can identify a group of architectural elements and professional practices that, when cultivated, enhance public well-being and when ignored detract from it, we may then begin to point to such elements as containing or improving the quality of publicness.

This possibility has not attracted much attention from scholars. Recognizing the force of neoliberal economics on the production of public space (or what passes for it these days), and largely unimpressed with the marginal improvements made possible by pro bono work, a new unsentimental pragmatic attitude toward the public good has asserted itself in the architectural academy. Not wishing to be taken in by mere nostalgia for a time that never really existed, Harvard Graduate School of Design Dean Sarah Whiting expresses with ill-disguised disdain:

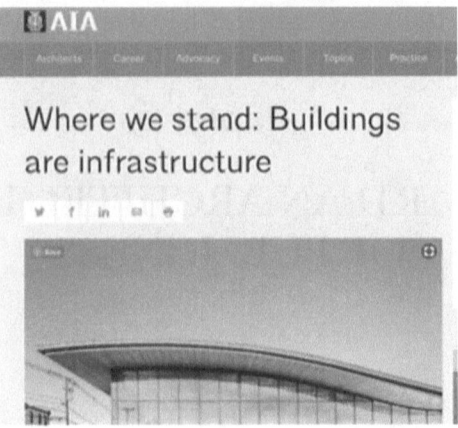

Figure 5.1 American Institute of Architects, September 12, 2017
Source: The American Institute of Architects, fair use

Lament-drenched, postlapsarian narratives about a lost public sphere […] invariably feed futile "retrieve and recover" missions that share success/failure rates with other contemporary missions based on myths. The public sphere in the US has, from its inception, been tied as much, if not more, to business than to its presumptive origin in government or some variant of public organisation.[1]

Whiting uses the term Bottom Line Public Spaces (BLPS) to identify public and pseudo-public spaces created by business interests. She thinks these have long been and are likely to continue to be the only public spaces created in the United States. BLPS "dot the entirety of American urbanism and are very likely the only hope for public space that we will see in the near future."[2] This new pragmatism toward the public realm seems to see only two choices, as Dana Villa observes: "It is the choice between a politics of mourning and a politics of parody, a politics that remembers the *res publica* and a politics engaged in the endless subversion of codes."[3]

Margaret Crawford's examination of the informal public realm of Los Angeles takes it as a nonstarter that the actions of architects do anything at all to create, reinforce, or redirect a public amenity. Instead, she concentrates on street vendors and other grassroots appropriations of public space out of government-owned (such as streets and sidewalks) or privately owned property (such as parking garages): "The emergence of these new public spaces and activities in Los Angeles, shaped by lived experience more than built space, raises complex political questions about the meaning of economic participation and citizenship in our cities."[4] In the search for genuine grassroots public spaces, how is it possible that all the buildings that architects have a hand in making to create the urban environment are left completely out of the equation?

One reason is that discussion of the public realm easily elides into discussion of open, urban space among historians and sociologists as much as with architects. As much as we heard about the "internet revolution" during the Arab Spring, or the internet's role in the Occupy Wall Street movement, it was not until bodies place themselves in urban space in Cairo, Istanbul, or Wall Street that the critical capability of opposition movements is realized. But unfortunately, open urban space is rarely the architect's creation.[5] It is what is leftover from their primary function of creating buildings—and so once again the architect's contribution to the public good occurs mostly in the margins. The upshot is that the public good derived from architecture is spoken of as something tangential to architects' core activities. It's what happens in the interstices and around buildings, but the potential role of buildings themselves in creating and reinforcing a vibrant public realm is neglected. Thus, it is entirely reasonable, from this perspective, that both Margaret Crawford and Stan Allen would see more creative potential for shaping contemporary public space in the work of landscape architects and in the emerging field of landscape urbanism than in the work of architects.[6]

Furthermore, the expansion of the private realm has led to severely diminished expectations of the public and by extension, of what architects can do to beneficially influence it. The pragmatic determination to avoid nostalgia for a time that never really existed leads, ultimately, to the serious proposition by Dana Cuff that the public be rebranded merely as infrastructure:

> "communities"—particularly those located in suburbs—undermine anything resembling a coherent, cosmopolitan expression of collective identity. In contrast to these fragmented, local associations, designers must now try to wring a form of public architecture from those lowly infrastructures that transcend the local—sewers, storm water channels, power grids, highways, and rail lines.[7]

And so it has come to this. The prime opportunity remaining for architects in economically advanced Western societies to creatively engage the public is the sewer system. At least now we know what rock bottom looks like, because there can be no further to fall. But the appeal of the architecture-infrastructure equation has spread. Even such a celebrated architect as Thom Mayne appears persuaded: "I'm not giving up on design; it isn't an either/or. But the most compelling work in front of us today is infrastructural."[8] Perhaps impressed by Dana Cuff's suggestion, the American Institute of Architecture (AIA) has made "Buildings are infrastructure" a branding slogan in yet another confused attempt to associate architecture with something fundamental to the public good. But, just as in Cuff's suggestion, this is an idea best put aside. While it is obviously true that buildings have some features of infrastructure, reducing buildings to such a lowly ideal in our society does the cause of the public good no service.

The surface appeal of the architecture–infrastructure equation is that it neatly folds architecture into everyday life. Since buildings, like roads and drainage systems, are ubiquitous features of modernity, this formulation allows us to assert the importance of that necessary ubiquity. So, for example, it is an obvious truism that airports are part of a nation's infrastructure. But (and here we can quickly see the gap in meaning opening), what of their aspirational content? Aren't the airports that are conceived and built according to fluid efficiency diagrams (like the sewer system) the worst, not the best, airports? What of museums, houses, and schools? Do we really want to condemn them to machine-imagery informed efficiency? Indeed, "Buildings are infrastructure" would seem to offer little difference from a tired, discredited functionalism trotted out *one more time* if the commonplace meaning of the term is employed. This may be why the seemingly self-contradictory term "soft infrastructure" has gained currency. Soft infrastructure, according to Cathleen McGuigan, "includes urban design and landscape projects like parks and public plazas; facilities like libraries, health-care clinics and social housing; and more traditional infrastructure like local and regional mass transit."[9] This "softening" threatens to collapse the distinction between infrastructure and the institutional architecture sector in order to make it more palatable.

If we try to recast the term "infrastructure" to include a structure's artistic content, we run the risk of having stretched the concept beyond all recognition. A proponent of this approach might point at a handful of bridges and dams as being both infrastructure and beautiful to show that artistic content is not ruled out, but the point here is that bridges and dams are infrastructure whether beautiful or not, while buildings simply fail to be architecture without artistry entering the equation. A third option which preserves the common meaning of infrastructure: to assert that the importance of architecture consists in its role as infrastructure + something else (like art, etc.) appears to leave the situation just as complicated as it was found and so achieves nothing. We can do much better. We can forego "architecture is infrastructure" as an ill-conceived attempt at recovering lost relevance and instead cultivate architectural elements and norms of practice that contribute to publicness in the Habermasian and feminist senses and minimize those elements that discourage it. If publicness is a quality that buildings and places can have more or less of, then we should be able to identify elements that contribute to or discourage it. What follows is a set of ideas about how to encourage greater publicness in architecture and comparisons between buildings and public spaces of greater and lesser publicness.

Privately Owned Public Spaces (POPS)

While architects may have mostly indirect involvement in the production of government-owned urban space, they are likely to have a good deal more influence in the creation of privately owned public spaces, or POPS. "Many of the places in which Americans spend a lot of our time, places that may look and feel public, are, from a legal perspective, private."[10] The term "Privately Owned Public Space" may sound initially like a peculiarly American oxymoron, but these odd hybrid creatures have come into existence as a solution to the pressing need for public space in such dense cities as New York and San Francisco, when city governments are unable to budget for them. Cities, in effect, "pay" developers in the currency of increased floor-area-ratios or other valuable regulatory easing for carving out of their projects some public or quasi-public space and therefore these public spaces are direct products and outgrowths of architects' buildings. They are designed into the overall project. If architects devise such spaces with an eye toward their potential for improving city life for the many, then we can well assert that they are working for the public good. That this work often falls short is indicated by the *New York Times* identifying many of these POPS as examples of "hostile architecture."[11] While often an apt appraisal, its identification overlooks the many conceptual difficulties POPS both present and exemplify. Even after 50 years of implementation, there is still no consensus for what makes a good one, such is the diversity of uses and populations that any given POPS may serve. Researchers who have tried to quantify success in terms of the number of users during a given time period have been unable to strongly correlate utility with design measures that were hypothesized to encourage free use on one end of the spectrum or control for more narrowly prescribed uses on the other.[12] Jeremy Nemeth and Stephen Schmidt attempted to identify degrees of publicness, not along a single continuum, but against three different axes of users, ownership, and management. Even though they believe that any model of publicness must be "empirically quantifiable" if it is not to "dissolve into a set of anecdotes and personal observations," they were not able to create a convincing example of such a thing.[13] While defining success of such spaces presents deep conceptual difficulties, consensus does exist on the fact that use would be enhanced by a clearer statement of purpose of what these public-private arrangements are meant to achieve. As it stands, it's hard to say when such a space doesn't hold up its end of the bargain. Since its goals are poorly defined, this arrangement is often perceived as not paying-off for the public. While it is easy to point at developers and private property owners as the bad guys, it has been observed that city-owned public spaces engage in the same strategies of control (controlled hours, surveillance, barriers to sleeping, set-asides for consumers) as do private owners. Concerns about social equity apply just as readily to government-owned spaces as they do to the privately owned.

A more nuanced understanding of the situation may help all concerned devise a theory of POPS that can be widely applied. No inherent contradiction is entailed by the private ownership of public space. The contradiction begins to arise when we equate private ownership with for-profit ownership that indeed does contain built-in conflicts. Profit maximization and public good, while not necessarily mutually exclusive, have success criteria with only some overlap. As argued in Chapter 2, the public and its good are not reducible to market mechanisms. If we agree that public spaces cannot be devised to accommodate whatever action people may come up with, that they must, in fact, be devised to accommodate some limited set of possible activities, and if we further acknowledge that they exist in the absence of full city government support leaving their owners responsible for their policing, then the conflict is not between rapacious development and people without economic clout, but instead over types of use: POPS owners must try to limit the range of possible uses (as campgrounds or as skate parks, for example) while individuals, in the absence of a clear understanding of the purpose of such places, will inevitably test those limits. "Anti-homeless spikes" placed on railings and benches by their private owners in New York are a case in point.[14] The homeless, with nowhere in the city that welcomes them, can be predicted to appropriate any flat surface that is sheltered from traffic. Spikes are seen by homeless advocates as attempts to stigmatize "undesirables" and wish away the problem rather than help solve it, and there is truth in this assertion. But neither can parks, benches, and walls be used for encampments without rapid degradation and ultimately negation of their usefulness for many others. The problem lies, not in the fact that sleeping is a discouraged activity in such places (because it is not possible that they be devised to accommodate every conceivable activity), but that the activities they were designed to accommodate and what they exclude are poorly conceived on the design end and hard to perceive on the use end. Misunderstanding and resentment are the unsurprising outcomes.

Lacking widespread consensus on just what such public spaces should accommodate, Jeremy Németh says that, "Bonus space managers implement robust combinations of techniques to control who uses a space and how."[15] Some POPS attempt to ameliorate this situation by posting detailed rules of conduct, but these postings can be hard to find or if plainly visible, largely ignored. People understandably do not see the need to read the instructions before proceeding with their everyday lives. Indeed, "there is no explicit or commonly shared definition of exclusiveness or how it should be measured."[16] Furthermore, this problem is not restricted to POPS but even applies to government-administered sidewalks, squares, and parks. They are easily overwhelmed by uses for which they were not designed, to the dismay of everyone. Families understandably abandon playgrounds where needles can be found, people will go to some lengths to avoid sidewalks that have become toilets, outdoor restaurant seating inhibits pedestrian flow, and so on. Conflict between owners' intentions and some individuals' actions is the predictable result. In recognition of the built-in conflict and the conceptual vagueness attached to them, a more robust understanding of the sorts of activities POPS should be designed to accommodate is needed. At least one set of observers concurs. After praising the diversity of uses and populations they observed in indoor New York POPS, Te-Sheng Huang and Karen A. Franck concluded in their study that the City "needs to provide more specific and consistent interpretation of rules of conduct for the private corporations and institutions that own and manage bonus spaces just as they do for required design features."[17] Applying the criteria for a well-functioning bourgeois public realm to public space may be a useful start. Such spaces would be unprogrammed enough to allow for self-organizing activity—not infinitely diverse, but somewhat diverse—and these diverse uses would not all reduce to consumer activities—some would be market externalities. Only if these criteria were met would we know that a public space had been produced.

Emptiness

Among the fundamental characteristics of the public is that it is self-organized. Therefore, for a space to be public, its use cannot be fully determined, it cannot be fully consumed nor fully amortized for profit for it must allow for the unprogrammed or unplanned. Making room for individual initiative in our buildings runs counter to a strand of modernist thinking that tends toward the highly prescriptive. Minimalism, for example, is easily spoiled by clutter and by sentimental attachment to things. To live harmoniously with a minimalist house is quite demanding. Even though minimal spaces may appear empty, they have the wrong kind of emptiness. The kind of emptiness needed for a space to have true publicness derives from a diagnosis of contemporary architecture by Michael Benedikt, who asserts that architecture has increasingly become about experience. The experience economy is something of a shark, endlessly chewing through new experiences in search of happiness, requiring constant movement to avoid decline. Benedikt opposes the privileging of experience as the measure of architecture's ultimate good with the idea of an architecture of reality, one that combines the necessary ingredients of presence, significance, materiality, and emptiness.

By "emptiness" Benedikt means "a building's lack of didacticism, a sort of indifference and generosity that we can't or don't want to explain."[18] A building's emptiness allows room for user interpretation. The space of possible experience or use is not preordained. Interpretation is not rigorously manipulated. This idea of architecture's "emptiness" may point the way for works of architecture to effectively oppose diminishing marginal returns and join forces with the opposition hoping for a justification for the act of architectural design beyond the reward and punishment of the market. A building's or an urban space's "emptiness" is precisely what makes it difficult to capitalize. If you cannot spell out in advance what the likely use is to be, and therefore the likely users, then you cannot market it.

Consider, for example, the space of the Capitol Mall in Washington, DC. Given the law of diminishing marginal returns that operates on the value of experience, one would expect that, through use, its value (the regard in which it is held and the significance it holds to Americans) would diminish

Figure 5.2 The Capitol Mall, Washington, DC
Source: Tom Spector

over time, just as the thrill of a new car or a roller-coaster ride diminishes. Having hosted civil rights marches and Martin Luther King Jr.'s stirring oration, the AIDS quilt demonstration, the million-man march, and many other events during its history, we would expect it to be regarded as partially, if not wholly used up: March somewhere more interesting next time. But just the opposite is the case. The civil rights marches and AIDS quilts have only added to the resonance of the place and the value it holds in the minds of many Americans. It has *increased* in meaning and value through use, not decreased. The same holds for a myriad of public places: Rockefeller Center, The Hollywood Bowl, Golden Gate Park. These places' "emptiness" to expressions of public interpretation keep them young, from an economic point of view. Marketplace economics simply hasn't the tools to account for the kind of value that doesn't wear out, become obsolete, depreciate, or become otherwise consumed. Architecture, however, does. The grand archway at Rowe's Wharf, in Boston, provides just such an empty space. It provides a portal to the waterfront, a grandly scaled welcome to the city, and an open, unprogrammed space for public use.

This particular kind of emptiness that leaves itself open to public interpretation exhibits the quality of publicness. A building or part of the built environment has publicness to the degree it encourages and allows unanticipated interpretations and to the degree it serves benefits external to itself. Publicness in architecture is a quality that facilitates or encourages self-organized interpretation of the built environment. Guides are neither required nor desired. Openness to the unanticipated is the only possible defense against diminishing marginal returns because, no matter the ingenuity of the architect to anticipate possible uses and interpretations, eventually the ability to anticipate, mold, and channel interpretation will give out. Upon achievement of this eventuality, staleness of experience sets in, thus diminishing its value. Through its publicness, however, the built environment stands to be continuously reinvigorated.

Politics

Public space as the crucial venue for political action is implied in the earlier discussion but the political is accommodated in other ways too. The concept of publicness provides some measure for finding commonalities among such counterpublics as the Sierra Club, Architecture for Humanity, Occupy Wall Street, Habitat for Humanity, Public Architecture and Architecture 2030. By implication, if not always by explicit attempt, each attacks the primacy of the private, whether it is the primacy of consumption over participation, the privileging of private experience, private ownership, personal autonomy, or the privatization

Figure 5.3 The Archway at Rowes Wharf, Boston, SOM architects
Source: Tom Spector

of the good. This is where the architecture of consumerism's opponents, despite their diversity, all line up. Each in its own way rehabilitates an aspect of the concept of the public good. The environmental movement encourages discarding the subjectivity of consumerism by giving new status to the Earth as something with an objective dignity or value. A building's or space's publicness stands to help prolong the use of that which is already in place and thus it is potentially another arrow in its quiver of concepts for helping forestall ecological catastrophe. It also stands to aid in bringing people together in ways that ultimately transcend the pursuit of individual self-interest, and this can only be to the good for the environmental movement.

A building with real publicness also facilitates the prospect of greater equity in the built environment, as it encourages the formerly marginalized to become an empowered part of the whole. It serves social justice in a way that buildings which speak only of power and domination cannot. The possibility of coming together to possess a place like the Capitol Mall, if only for a while, makes pragmatist philosopher John Dewey's vision of an aesthetic democracy of highly engaged citizenry palpable.[19]

It may seem suspect to laud the unbridled good embodied in the publicness of the Capitol Mall following the repellent events that took place in the U S Capitol and in the Capitol Mall on January 6, 2020 (as this book was in its final stages of editing). But there is plenty of reason to demur from this suspicion. Depending on one's outlook, either a self-organized group of thugs convened itself to thwart democracy, or else a seeming public (of appearance but not of substance) was relentlessly manipulated into existence by one group of elites and exhorted into thinking they were there to save a stolen election from an undemocratic conspiracy hatched by a different group of elites. Either way, thugs or dupes, the people that took over the Capitol that day cannot be claimed to be part of a public according to the definition taken from Habermas. If they were manipulated into existence, then they were not self-organizing. If they were self-organizing, then they were distinctly uninterested in engaging in anything resembling public discourse. That the events that day should not be attributed to a pathology of the public sphere may be small comfort to those who suffered, but it should at least allow us to forego letting those events cast a shadow over a valuable idea.

The aesthetic democracy can, and should, have an intimate connection with public space. Harvard philosopher Michael Sandel observes that "Public spaces, such as these (schools, workplaces, churches, synagogues, and in trade unions and social movements) were indispensable to the finest expression of republican politics in our time, the civil rights movement of the 1950s to mid-1960s."[20] The civil rights movement undertook the formative project of the transformation of a people. This "formative aspect of republican politics requires public spaces that gather citizens together, enable them to interpret their condition, and cultivate solidarity and civic engagement."[21] The publicness of our buildings allows for the development of particular identities in association with particular places. For the civil rights movement, this development of identity came out of the public spaces provided by the Black churches of the South.

In the aesthetic democracy, aesthetic value emerges, not through the passive experience of taking in and savoring sensations, but through active participation. Unlike taste, value is a public affair, and also unlike taste, it is oriented outward—toward putting oneself out into the world—rather than inward, of making oneself a repository for the most exquisite discriminations. In the pragmatist conception, one comes to know oneself only through interaction with the world. In a sensory deprivation chamber, there is no self, or at least one cannot know if there is a self or not. Similarly with art. One comes to know of art and aesthetic value by the rich and various ways in which one can interact with it, not by how thoroughly one can isolate and purify the experience of it. This pragmatist conception is particularly good news for architecture, which is the most immersive medium possible, encompassing as it does, not just the eyes or ears, but the whole body in a huge variety of situations. Out of participation emerges both meaning and value, and Dewey was right to invoke the example of the Greeks, despite the differences in their concept of the public from ours. It hardly seems a coincidence that a society that enjoyed the most intense public participation also enjoyed intense aesthetic development of the built environment. Our isolating and savoring of Greek art and architecture can only impart a nearly colorless echo of that public world into which one could throw oneself in intense participation. Only in built environments of real publicness is this possible. In these places and spaces, people are encouraged to invent how they will participate.

The Deweyan conception of knowing through participation fits well with and reinforces the feminist insistence that we must always consider our situated, embodied selves. To the degree that works of architecture are public, the ultimately empowering risk-taking of placing the body in public view allows architecture to become a force for social justice, instead of its all-too-familiar role as enforcer of the social status quo. Whether serving for a march on the Capitol Mall, or the enjoyment of a concert at the Hollywood Bowl, the publicness of architectural space is relentlessly not the disembodied public of letters or, now, the internet. It is where people risk exposure of their full humanity and not just the edited versions they want others to see. In truly public environments, not only is public interpretation of architecture open-ended, but public interpretation of itself is too. The built environment is the most powerful venue yet devised for public self-interpretation. It is neither replaceable nor interchangeable with anything else in this regard.

Appropriation

As a basic value or justification for architecture, publicness operates in design thinking much like the Vitruvian values of utility, durability, and beauty in that it too is a "thick" concept that combines descriptive and normative content. Holding publicness to be an essential ingredient of architecture would help make sense of the difficulty in evaluating the architectural merit of built environments in narrowly controlled situations, such as at theme parks.

Benedikt argues that the lack of Disney's Main Street, USA's "emptiness" is what prevents it from becoming real architecture. This conclusion presumes the ability to judge the real from unreal, which may be assuming too much in such situations. Employing the measure of publicness, instead, leads to a different sort of conclusion. It leads to the conclusion that with built environments as thoroughly controlled and manipulated as Main Street, USA, we can never know whether they are architecture or not, real or unreal. Disney's foreclosure of public interpretation, unlike in main streets across the country, leaves us lacking the conceptual tools for determining its status at all, much less whether it is good, bad, or indifferent. On the postmodernist question of whether Main Street, USA is good or bad architecture, the answer is: We have no way of knowing. You can't even legally publish a photo of it. Because it lacks the quality of publicness and instead narrowly constrains the space of possible interpretation, because it lacks open-endedness to interpretation, judgment is not possible. It is forever deferred. This makes Main Street, USA the most fantastic and subversive of all Disney's creations, because it careens so close to something real and public, intimating publicity but never quite crossing that line. But its status as a private good also makes it entirely subject to diminishing returns.

Figure 5.4 Oklahoma City, Bricktown
Source: Tom Spector

In contrast, the area of Oklahoma City known as Bricktown began its life as a themed space intended to subvert all readings of authenticity but has since transmuted into something more. Even its name suggests theming. What was initially a grim loading alley for vacant multistory brick warehouses was dredged, refocused, filled with water, and rebranded into a tourist attraction modeled on San Antonio's Riverwalk. Which buildings are original? Which are new? What elements are authentic to the place? Which create ersatz history? Making sense of these questions is nearly impossible and not even worth the trouble. But early in its history something interesting began to happen to Bricktown. While the area was only a marginal success as a tourist attraction, it began to be taken up as a valued extension of downtown by the locals. Offices and housing moved in. Its initial boundaries softened and expanded. People began using Bricktown in various unplanned and piecemeal ways: as a place to kill a few minutes, have a picnic, meet friends, even to work and live. Through public appropriation, Bricktown became, against the odds, a real place and not just a carefully curated tourist attraction.

Encouraging a sense of public possession of the built environment, however, runs counter not only to the societal trends discussed earlier, but also counter to a persistent strand of thought in contemporary architecture that encourages control, mastery, and aesthetic denial, and which discourages open-ended interpretation. Architects are all too familiar with the disappointment that sets in when someone other than the original client moves in and fails to appreciate the proper way of inhabiting a building; the way it was designed for. We are all, furthermore, acutely aware of the carefully framed, cropped, and furnished views of works of architecture held to contain the correct vantage point. The quality of publicness must discourage any such idea as a "correct vantage point" or a "proper" way to inhabit. Architecture with this quality would have to, instead, be generous enough to facilitate others to make up entirely new narratives using the architecture as a prop. Prolonging a building's value then would no longer depend on how cleverly misuse is precluded. It would depend more on the architect's ability to negotiate "limitless democratic vistas" (to borrow a phrase from Richard Rorty) of public reinterpretation within a building or space that is borne, of necessity, out of a certain ideology. The architect's role in providing for publicness through appropriation becomes the balancing of the definite and the indeterminate, the teleological with the openness of ends.

Public Face

Publicness, then, embodies an attitude of generosity toward appropriation by others, but it also may take on objective architectural characteristics that

Figure 5.5 San Francisco Federal Building, Morphosis and Smithgroup architects
Source: Tom Spector

are made most evident when they are peculiarly absent. The San Francisco Federal Building, designed by Morphosis (with SmithGroup Architects) and completed in 2007, likely heralds a new age in public buildings in the United States at a time when the concept of "public building" needs a reboot. The result of a "unique combination of avant-garde formal autonomy and political engagement" whose appearance was largely justified by sustainability objectives, it exemplifies an approach that stands to help the architecture profession overcome its relegation to the status of "weak service provider," in educator Sylvia Lavin's dismissive turn-of-phrase in a critique of the building.[22] Many in the field of architecture are pinning their hopes on sustainability to provide both a formal agenda and a strong moral mission for contemporary architecture, but this is unlikely to be a complete solution because sustainability is better thought of as a means than as an end in itself. After all, there

Figure 5.6 Salt Lake City Federal Courthouse, Thomas Phifer architects
Source: Tom Spector

is no logical conflict between a building's being both perfectly dreadful and meeting many targets of sustainability. Its sustainability credentials certainly have not insulated the Federal Building from controversy over its imposing, yet mute appearance on Mission Street. The liabilities of the approach to form-making illustrated by the Federal Building suggests that we could also pay attention to what we might call a building's public face—and here the work of architects is incredibly influential. The public face of a building—that it implicitly acknowledges the needs of a public to make sense of what is going on inside—is particularly crucial with government buildings. Sadly, this idea is hardly acknowledged these days.

Certainly, the idea that our government buildings should have a public face—one that acknowledges the existence of humans inside as well as outside appears to not even be a consideration any longer, if the much lauded and published San Francisco Federal building is any indication. Here, the ability to sense human occupants inside that a public outside might have some vested interested in perceiving doesn't even seem to be part of the thinking where human scale and any sense of individuality behind the screen seems to be methodically erased. And this is no aberration. The even newer U.S. District Courts building in Salt Lake City by Thomas Phifer and Partners Architects does much the same thing. Is it any wonder that locals nicknamed it the Borg building after a famous series of episodes in *Star Trek: The Next Generation*? Once again, all sense of individuals inhabiting the building is methodically erased. It is a design that is not hard to read as the product of fear of exposure to the public instead of as proud touchstone *for* the public. This lack of legibility doesn't even seem to be a talking point in the published reviews which mostly covered it in glowing terms.

Buildings such as the San Francisco Federal Building and the Salt Lake City U.S. Courts that erase all signs of human habitation within or sense of human scale without are disregarding the public's need to mentally inhabit context in order to make sense of it and, more pointedly, to be able to intuit the existence of well-meaning humans at work within its government buildings. The metallic screen covering the south wall of the Federal Building could hardly speak louder of impervious, faceless, panoptic bureaucracy. The people inside, *if* there are people inside, can survey the public, but the public can have no sense of the building's inhabitants. This disregard for a government building's public face makes sense if there is no significant public to face. In yet another sign of the fallen fortunes of the concept of publicness, this observation has largely escaped mainstream architectural criticism. Though a neglected idea today (Blondel was promoting this in the eighteenth century as the concept of *caractère*), a building's public face and form can contribute mightily to the public's sense of ownership, belonging, and orientation. Indeed, as Lavin asserted in a well-known essay on Quatremère de Quincy,

> mechanisms that encouraged and required standards both of literacy and legibility were built into and enabled the very notion of a public space. And while paradigms of cultivated taste and of architectural legibility have changed since the eighteenth century, their use as evaluative criteria in assessing the publicness of architecture, and of the spaces it defines, remains almost uncontested.[23]

Uncontested and yet, also, apparently, too dowdy to be of any creative interest.

A building's public face is concerned with an inner quality, and one that has a teleology. Though this exact formulation of this sort of quality in a building was not expressed by Vitruvius, the same idea is at work in his insistence on a building's appropriateness; that it expresses a countenance, level of finish and ornament, and grandeur or humility appropriate to its owner's public station in life and to the building's public function. While Vitruvius' concept presumes and encourages what we would take to be a repellent social stratification, it at the same time presumes and encourages social obligation as well. Vitruvius was not a social progressive and his ideals were bound to reflect this fact. But it is apparent that from its earliest formulation, architecture's public role was acknowledged. This recognition appears repeatedly in architecture's major texts. Leon Battista Alberti thought it a terribly important matter, the French pick up on this in the eighteenth century (beginning with Germain Boffrand and carried on by Blondel's[24]) insistence that assembling a building's *caractère*, its expressive function, was a major design task. This concern with creating an adequate public expression troubled modernism as well. J. J. P. Oud worried over the possibility of a "new monumentality" insisting that functionalism had been proven to be inadequate for the task.[25] But it has only been since World War II that the public realm has been in such full-fledged retreat from the rise of consumerism, procedural democracy, and privatization that the question of architecture's publicness could be thrown into such high relief.

The blankness and superhuman proportions of the Federal Building stand in stark contrast to another government building, San Francisco's City Hall, only a few blocks away. City Hall, with its hierarchical neoclassical composition building on a central rotunda provides all the elements missing at the Federal Building. Members of the public, even those not schooled in classicism, can read the façade and the form for visual cues. One can well imagine where the important offices are, where council meetings are held, where to enter and what windows to protest outside of; all signs of which are deliberately erased in the Federal Building.

San Francisco City Hall bespeaks of the grandeur of local democracy: The Federal Building reads as a technological instantiation of the leviathan justified in the name of sustainability. The "paradigms of cultivated taste and architectural legibility" have been lost here, but hopefully not for all time. Perhaps this example can serve as a caution to pay attention to architecture's public face as one component of serving the public good.

Scale

Roughly similar buildings in function may succeed or fail in the quality of their publicness because of their handling of scale. In San Francisco the forecourt of the Academy of Sciences building by Renzo Piano positively invites activity. Whereas the similarly functioning building by Calatrava in Valencia, Spain, is impossible to enliven due to its dwarfing scale. We see much the same at the British National Library in London which manages the scale of its entry with many intimate areas inviting reading or relaxing outside just beyond the main traffic noise of the King's Cross neighborhood. Contrast this

Figure 5.7 San Francisco City Hall
Source: Tom Spector

with the dwarfing, windswept scale at the French counterpart, the *Bibliothèque Nationale* in Paris.[26]

The many variables that must be manipulated to achieve appropriate scale lend it a strongly subjective cast. But observations of appropriate scale are not entirely subjective. Its beneficial manipulation depends on the number of people who can reasonably be expected to use a building or space, on climatic variables, on neighboring buildings, and on an initial list of activities to be encouraged. It is hard to speculate what activities were envisioned for the plaza of the *Biblioteque Nationale,* except, perhaps, hurrying.

Everyday Nobility

The grandeur of the Oculus at the World Trade Center in New York, the way it ennobles the simple act of passing through Lower Manhattan's transit hub, stands in extreme contrast to the mean proportions of the unphotographable second Pennsylvania Station in midtown Manhattan. But we do not have make such extreme comparisons to promote the idea that dignified office building lobbies, generously scaled entrances, or even overhangs and projections that

Figure 5.8 California Academy of Sciences, San Francisco, Renzo Piano Workshop, architects
Source: Rosangela Perry, Shutterstock.com photo ID: 682273117

temporarily shield pedestrians from the rain can be conceived within a spirit of generosity that exceeds consumption and financial gain. The middle-class value placed on the work that dignifies a person, which is a source of both community and moral uplift deserves its architectural corollary and cannot be reduced to mere efficiency. The more that a place which custom dictates be outfitted for mere utility—a public restroom, for example—instead shows the existence of a person who cared, the more it adds to the meaning of one's day-to-day world. This may well be a welcome extension of the feminist care ethic into the public realm. There are so many leftover spaces, Junkspaces, in Rem Koolhaus's memorable term, that we are not even supposed to notice *are* spaces, but which we nevertheless inhabit regularly: parking lots and garages, corridors, and the like, that would benefit from even small changes by caring architects, which, cumulatively, would make enormous differences in peoples' lives.

Serving the Public though Making the Profession More Accountable

The search for the public good of architecture is two-pronged. It is a search for enhanced publicness in the built environment, and it is a search for enhanced

TOWARD AN ARCHITECTURE OF PUBLICNESS   127

Figure 5.9 City of Arts and Sciences, Valencia, Santiago Calatrava, architect
Source: Tom Spector

public responsiveness within the profession. The profession's promotional and governing organizations, the AIA and NCARB in the United States, the RIBA and ARB in the United Kingdom, are well-placed to promote the public good by taking measures to strengthen the architecture profession. The following are proposals for encouraging greater architect control and accountability.

1. Taking Control of Cost

Approximately 70 percent of architects' projects in the United States meet their cost and schedule targets. While this may not seem such a terrible statistic, if 30 percent of an airline's flights overshot the runway, people would soon seek more reliable carriers. Architects' inability to more reliably forecast project costs may bear some debt to the antibourgeois disdain for too much concern about money discussed in Chapter 1. This inability is certainly the opening giving rise to the construction management (CM) trade. The situation could begin to be reversed by creating a comprehensive, cloud-based database of construction component costing for the exclusive use of the organizations'

Figure 5.10 British National Library, London, Colin St. John Wilson, architect
Source: Tom Spector

members. Inroads have begun along these lines with the developing interoperability between the R. S. Means cost guides, Revit cost schedules and Uniformat construction assemblies. Though limited in scope now, attaching costs to elements in a comprehensive BIM model could, when detailed enough, allow architects to regain control ceded to construction management (CM) firms and quantity surveyors for the ultimate betterment, not just of conditions of practice, but also for their projects. The AIA and the RIBA, through the participation of members, could quickly scale-up cost profiles of almost any construction assembly through the development of a master database. The firm's cost of access to the database could be simply

Figure 5.11 *Biblioteque Nationale*, Paris, Dominique Perrault, architect
Source: Tom Spector

met by contributing to the knowledge base. Architects' inability to predict and control costs has perhaps been the single largest source of discontent for clients as well as the single largest source of erosion of authority. Placing CM-dominated construction cost and sequencing information into the BIM model, instead of, as is common now, handing things over to them, places their work in the proper subordinate role (if they are still needed at all) with the architect remaining in charge. With easy access to comprehensive construction cost information, cost models can be built up as the BIM develops, and adjusted dynamically as the model adjusts—as much a part of everyday practice as verifying area calculations. Greater cost control brings greater leverage in the construction equation and, ultimately, greater control over the quality of the product.

2. Enacting Basic Public Protections

Architects' commitments to meeting all sorts of codes and land use restrictions in our work is a basic category of publicness. Fire safety is an obvious example of a public good that cannot be fully capitalized by the market. While adequate exits, rated enclosures, and fire sprinkler systems can be expected to accrue to a building's value in the marketplace in terms of lowered insurance premiums

Figure 5.12 The Oculus, World Trade Center, New York, Santiago Calatrava, architect

and heightened rental rates, the external benefits that accrue to neighboring buildings, passersby, and the city at large cannot be charged out for the benefit of the owner. But neither does the government own it. At the same time, the standards for fire safety are explored and promoted to local governments by such paradigmatic public entities as the National Fire Protection Association (NFPA). The entire concept of the building code is predicated on the idea that market forces alone will not suffice to provide basic building safety, and that the profit motive must be augmented by the complicated apparatus we know as code compliance and review. As important as it is, however, merely meeting codes is not good enough. If the best you can say about your building is that it meets all applicable codes, then not only haven't you aimed very high, but you are also leaving the important work of architecture to something that can in principle be programmed. Indeed, automated code compliance routines have been successfully tested and placed in trials.

3. Eliminating Free Work

Engaging in unpaid or poorly paid competitions for design commissions in effect allows the aristocrats to stage a jousting match with the design commission, instead of a damsel, as prize. Work on such competitions justify, in the minds of their participants, not paying or underpaying the young associates working for them. This outlook might not be coercive if unpaid work were offered as both optional and as a way to enjoy a piece of the profits, but such is never the case. A bourgeois, transaction-oriented, way of doing business thrives on the simple expectation of fee for service. NCARB's Model Rules of Conduct, placed into law in many U S jurisdictions, states

> 4.4 An architect shall neither offer nor make any payment or gift with the intent of influencing an official's judgment in connection with a prospective or existing project in which the architect is interested.

Just what sort of official is not named, but there is no reason to think that officials should be limited to those in government. Thus, architects which give away free work to developers and corporations (excluding legitimate pro bono work for nonprofit organizations) in addition to governments, in hopes of securing a job place themselves in something of a bind. Either they have to admit that their design work has no value, or else that they are attempting bribery. This is probably the most poorly enforced regulation among the rules of conduct, but if it were enforced, it would be to the betterment of all concerned.

4. Making use of Scientific Research

Architects are the last holdouts of the learned professions against specialization. This is not to say that there aren't specialized specifications writers, façade consultants and lighting designers and such, but the role "architect," presumably for both business as well as for ideological purposes, resists specialization in a way that would perplex the medical profession. This resistance in turn means that there is limited use and limited demand for scientific research into the presumptions, premises, and design methods that might be beneficially employed if some system of board certification existed. The result is that much design wisdom is based on rules of thumb with little empirical testing to back it up. Some inroads, however, have been made. LEED certification is a type of specialized designation, albeit one that is fairly easily obtained. To a small degree, specialization is already occurring as something of a pilot test in the field of healthcare architecture. The American College of Healthcare Architects (ACHA) does provide a specialized designation to established practitioners in this specialty and it is perhaps no surprise that the first inroads in architectural specialization would occur in an area already known to be friendly to it. So far, the AIA has avoided the controversy of either endorsing or dismissing this initiative. But perhaps the time has come to begin to evaluate its legacy and determine if future specialization is warranted. The ability to specialize on the basis of science-based and highly technical knowledge in a field, such as health care, stands to promote research into building performance that will feed a virtuous circle of enhanced knowledge leading to better performance which in turn promotes the prestige of the specialized practitioners which then encourages more research.

5. Respecting Employees

The AIA, NCARB, RIBA, and ARB are to be congratulated for the enthusiasm with which they have taken measures in recent years to strengthen the architecture profession's stand against workplace harassment and discrimination of all types, but some obvious further measures remain to be implemented. It is well within these organization's abilities and purview to actually state and make certification dependent on following the fair employment practices that should apply to all firms in their employment of their young associates. The cycles of young associate employment abuse and discouragement for women to advance has got to end. Firms that do want to treat their employees fairly are put at a competitive disadvantage by firms that do not.

Fair labor standards have been in effect in the United States since the 1930s. The basic outlines of these standards, therefore, should be well known.

Two well-known abuses, in particular, should be eliminated as a feature of architectural employment. First, firms should not be allowed to avoid employment taxes and insurance by hiring young future architects as independent subcontractors when in most cases, they simply do not meet the test. Second, many young associates will not meet the creative professional exemption from overtime pay, and therefore, are deserving of time-and-a-half for work exceeding 40 hours per week. The particularities of these requirements should be spelled out, publicized, and policed by our professional organizations.

Architects' organizations should produce advisory papers instructing firms of all sizes and degrees of prestige on the legal treatment of employees. Firms that insist on skirting these requirements should be hounded out of business. Victims of illegal employment practices will be much more likely to blow the whistle on their abusers, if they perceive the existence of a professional organization that will vigorously stand up for them. By making the conditions of employment fairer, we stand to reduce the horribly inefficient attrition rates the profession suffers, while at the same time breeding exactly the kind of loyalty that helps build subsequent leadership as the architecture profession, for the first time ever, becomes a body of people similarly motivated to move architecture forward as the twenty-first century unfolds.

Climate Change and the Problem of Future Publics

In addition to furthering existing public goods, anthropogenic climate change introduces the vexing issue of the architecture profession also needing to consider how it is to serve future publics now. The problem of not-yet-existing publics functions as something of a stress test for moral theories. The moral novelty of anthropogenic catastrophes is that until the late twentieth century, we have been able to take for granted the notion that life would go on after we die. There was no question to Aristotle, or Kant or Mill but that humanity would continue after they were no more. But now, in its worst prospects, the climate change unleashed in the nineteenth century and continuing unchecked poses the terrifying possibility of mass extinction. This possibility throws many of our moral intuitions out the window. Samuel Scheffler points out that much about our moral lives can be explained by this expectation of human existence continuing long after we have departed this world. He invites us to consider what would ensue if we had certain knowledge of the destruction of all humanity shortly after our own natural deaths. Even though this future annihilation would have no effect on us now, we would still find that many of our current projects and values had become meaningless. Scheffler points out that many people routinely pursue goals, such as seeking a cure for cancer, or building a cathedral without the expectation that they will be achieved in their own lifetimes, and yet still find such goals and such pursuits worthwhile. The foreknowledge of life no longer going on after we are gone would cause us to have little care for these projects and, conversely, the prospect that future people would suffer due to our actions gives us good reason to care. Scheffler says that, "The prospect of the imminent disappearance of the race poses a far greater threat to our ability to treat other things as mattering to us, and, in so doing, it poses a far greater threat to our continued ability to lead value-laden lives."[27] Thus, people do routinely care about what happens in the future, even a future they may have no share in, but, with regard to climate change, the uncertainties about the doomsday allow room for selfish near-term calculations to enter. Scheffler's is an appealingly hopeful approach. The causal dependence of future generations on what we do now, far from being a burdensome obligation, he thinks can be seen as a welcome opportunity to have some influence in a matter we actually care greatly about despite the fact that we will not know the outcome. "There are actually things we can do to promote the survival and flourishing of humanity after our deaths, such as taking action to solve the problems of climate change."[28]

Others are considerably less hopeful. Environmental ethics scholar Dale Jamieson, assuming that the die is already cast, asks if it is surprising that "the largest collective action problem that humanity has ever faced, one that is extended both in space and time" was lost?[29] Climate change is such an unfamiliar situation to humanity that it "swamp(s) the machinery of morality."[30] The key elements of the perfect moral storm of climate change, according to philosopher Stephen Gardiner, are problems of agency, intergenerational buck-passing, and the inapplicability of existing political theories combining to create what he has termed the moral corruption of climate change.[31] Ethicist Clive Hamilton is even more pessimistic. Hamilton sees in the reticence to act when we know that action is necessary and can be effective as signs of moral abdication or moral collapse. His verdict: "Humanity's ethical impulse has dissipated."[32]

Thus, while the urgency of climate change is readily apparent, the morality of taking appropriate action is complex. As Matthew Coffay observes in his dissertation, standard consequentialist theories are not up to the challenge of climate change because they judge the wrongness of acts in light of their effects on already existing individuals and discount the effects on future, and therefore hypothetical, individuals.[33] The moral problems of deciding for future people (and future animals, for that matter) has occupied a small but distinct branch of moral philosophy even before climate change took center stage. Derek Parfit's discussion of the Identity Problem (also sometimes called the Non-Identity Problem) in an essay from 1983 "Energy Policy and the Further Future: The Identity Problem"[34] has proven influential on more recent climate ethics. The problem, especially for consequentialist and guilt-based ethics, is to determine exactly what we should hold ourselves guilty for and to whom. When it comes to climate change, guilt-based morality knows no bounds. The current generation is in danger of being the squeezed in the middle—a victim of past careless excess, and also obliged to the demands of the future. Guilt-based morality can make the problems of individual agency seem overwhelming: Should I quit cooking food altogether? Never take another flight? Become a vocal protestor? Park my car for good? Refrain from having children? Even if I lived in a way to ensure achieving net zero carbon emission, should I do more? This boundless guilt, even for things our generation did not cause, leads some writers to assert that applying a virtue-based ethic to the problem is the best alternative. It would certainly make current life more pleasant. Even posing the situation in terms of guilt-based morality to the public may well backfire and actually lead to inaction, as it has been shown that framing issues as moral obligations easily turns into defensive behavior. Framing a situation as, instead, a matter of competence, tends to make groups respond with action. According to Susanne Tauber, Martijn van Zomeren, and Maja Kutlaca, "Thus, there is a risk that the cognitive dissonance that people experience when thinking about climate change together with the moral framing that is common in public discourse actually unfold cumulative effects, resulting in psychological paralysis rather than in improvement and adjustment of behaviour."[35] The problems with determining moral action for the benefit of future others led Parfit to formulate the platitude that an action or policy is wrong if it makes things worse off for those who live in the future "than for those who might have lived,"[36] but how motivating is that?

It remains to be seen whether the exigencies of climate change will push architecture's other ethical dilemmas to the background. Some would say they already have, or at the least should have, even though plenty of urgent situations exist that would benefit from architects' leadership: homelessness, prisons, displacement due to gentrification, urban sprawl, and more besides. There is nothing terribly novel about the call for a profession to sometimes lead, instead of follow, its multiple publics through troubling times even though it has limited power to enforce such leadership. Undeniably, however, for a profession wishing to serve the public good, climate change creates the fresh questions of what the future good consists, how to promote it, and whether it renders other concerns less significant. The assumption made by many climate activists that we know what future publics would want of us has to be at least somewhat tempered by the fact that we often misread what *current* publics want of us. Is looking backwards to what we would have liked to have asked of the nineteenth century an adequate guide to looking forward to the twenty-second? If only people currently existing could be counted as reliable proxies for future people, then at least some of those dilemmas would evaporate.

Promoters of strong architectural leadership on climate change think that the current absence of top-down leadership (as is currently experienced in much of the English-speaking world), presents opportunities for the importance of a middle-out approach to assert itself. Members of the professional middle of society are the best situated to provide leadership downward to the public, guidance upward to the state and lateral cooperation with fellow providers.[37] The interim results, however, of the middle-out approach have not been encouraging. Architects have tried mightily to insert themselves into the climate change solution with limited effect. Middle-out action is possibly a good source of moral guidance but its ability to enforce action has as yet proven poor. Even if the middle-out approach proves effective, are we promoting the right thing? If, as many argue, we are past the point of mitigation strategies, then we should be focusing more efforts on preparing the public for adaptation to the inevitable.

The temptation to advocate for a strong, authoritarian approach in the face of democratic and market inaction is equally fraught. As Malcolm Bull says, "Insofar as we move beyond the tyranny of the contemporary, we invite other forms of dictatorship, and the hard-won battle of democracy to exclude its ideological rivals by establishing the present as the temporal locus of sovereignty is under threat."[38] Indeed, the problems of inequality brought on by climate change often bring out proposals resembling international communism: to each according to his needs, from each according to his means. Such approaches are likely to cause severe erosion of professional autonomy to act. Will and Cathy Hughes, for example, believe we will see the rise of "a new professionalism that requires less of professional institutions and more of the institutions of societal governance,"[39] and that this change may lead to a loss of individual professional agency when it is dissolved into something like bureaucracy. If a wartime authoritarianism works, but in the process removes our profession's independence, is it a small price to pay?

There are no great options here even though architects are probably more future-oriented than most people. Our professional lives are devoted to it. This accounts for why we care so much about flashing details. We welcome the prospect of working now for the benefit of future publics; it's the present one we have trouble with. Perhaps the least bad option, when it comes to climate change, is to arm ourselves with some of Scheffler's optimism, even while acknowledging that the doomsayers may be right.

Conclusion: The Next Structural Transformation of the Public Sphere

Habermas's account of the public sphere's transformation was decidedly pessimistic. From within, it was dissipating its normative strength and from without it was being undermined by private money and state bureaucratic power. This was in the early 1960s. Had *Structural Transformation* been written a decade later, following the 1960s tumult, he might well have had a different diagnosis—but one that would have been prematurely rendered. Once the 1960s activism was spent, the hollowing-out transformation of the public sphere resumed. He has left it to others to propose verdicts on its prospects today. But this pessimism in the short term should be weighed against his hopefulness for modernity in the long term that underlies all his writing. For Habermas, despite its failings, modernity provides the only path forward. The same goes for modernity's concomitant politics: liberal democracy. As Robert Kuttner has observed:

> Liberal democracy has endured a long history of premature burials by its detractors [...] It is troubling enough that autocracy is gaining ground in practice, but even more alarming that anti-liberalism is once again becoming reputable as theory. There is no good substitute for liberal democracy. All of the alternatives are even more corrosive of human dignity and personal virtue.[40]

Some 50+ years after *Structural Transformation* was published, it may well be appropriate to assert, as some authors have argued, that the public sphere has entered a second transformation—one as promising as it is treacherous. Evan Stewart and Douglas Hartmann have stated that,

> A second structural transformation has neither fully eliminated nor completely replaced existing institutions of civil society such as media organizations, institutions of higher education, or social movement organizations, and it has not eliminated conventional social practices of engaging the public sphere through those institutions. Instead, it has produced both new horizontal relationships for actors to access the public and new vertical relationships of power and influence.[41]

Stewart and Hartmann argue that the second structural transformation has been brought about by three developments: the rapid assembly and disassembly of multiple publics through electronic media, the professionalization of social movements, and the rising importance of public-private partnerships in the form of think-tanks, nonprofit foundations, inquiry centers and the like. I believe we should add the growing self-awareness of the ability of counterpublics to force recognition of their causes on the larger public and its governments to that list. From the Vietnam War, civil rights and nuclear power demonstrations in the 1960s, to ActUp! and gay pride, the recurrent iterations of Black Lives Matter, the Occupy movement, teachers' strikes, #metoo, to Tahrir and Taksim squares and the Hong Kong umbrellas, publics and counterpublics continue to self-organize in urban space and address themselves to power. Although electronic media has been crucial to the ability to quickly assemble and dissemble these publics, despite gushy pronouncements of social media enabling new virtual town squares, of adding to ever-increasing democratic vistas, what we have found instead is that virtual urban space is no substitute for the real thing—that there are no real stakes and no change occurs until actual bodies are assembled. Now that the presence of the body is made optional for public assembly by social media, we have discovered the importance of what used to be a backdrop condition. Should architects wish to realize the fullest implication of serving the public good, they will want to realize the power of architecture as a backdrop, as a setting and even as an agent for these newly creative outlets of public engagement with the world. And they will want to organize themselves to be ready to produce beneficial responses that facilitate public expression.

The necessity of embodied participation for the existence of a functioning public sphere was not anticipated by Habermas—its existence was assumed rather than argued for. At the time of its original publication in German in 1962, *The Structural Transformation of the Public Sphere* simply could not anticipate the stresses on public life introduced by internet-based social media. And so, even though recognizing its inability to account for these developments can hardly be a criticism, it is nevertheless a lack in need of further development. Habermas's neglect of the body, or of the embodied, was an outgrowth of his emphasis on the role of communicative rationality—as he liked to put it: the unforced force of the better argument—to anchor our moral commitments to one another. It is easy to see how his concepts led to this bias. For Habermas, the ideal of public discourse bracketed differences in social status, in inherited privileges, and in physical prowess. Rational argumentation was, ideally, mind to mind. Thus, the bodily, or the embodied, was deliberately down-played. But what he was unable to anticipate was the existence of an untethered realm of discourse on the internet in which arguments are interminable, incivility has no consequences, and claims to truth are strategically asserted. Western culture's ongoing experiment in digital social media as a public platform in the form of Facebook, Twitter and the like have now been around long enough that the extravagant early enthusiasm for new possibilities of rational public debate they make possible has dimmed considerably. As Annalee Newitz has observed:

> Collectively, they (Facebook and Twitter) gave me a glimpse of a future where the greatest tragedy is not the loss of our privacy. It is the loss of an open public sphere. There are many paths beyond the social media hellscape, and all of them begin with reimagining what it means to build public spaces where people seek common ground.

And further, that

> Public life has been irrevocably changed by social media; now it's time for something else. We need to stop handing off responsibility for maintaining public space to corporations and algorithms—and give it back to human beings. We may need to slow down, but we've created democracies out of chaos before. We can do it again.[42]

Newitz thinks the public square or public forum metaphor under which Facebook promotes itself is inherently misleading. It's a public square only if a public square were overflowing with chaos and, especially, anonymity. She thinks that we can rebuild "our damaged public sphere by creating digital public places that imitate actual town halls, concert venues and pedestrian-friendly sidewalks. These are places where people can socialize or debate with a large community, but they can do it anonymously. If they want to, they can just be faces in the crowd, not data streams loaded with personal information."[43] Thus, an interesting difference between virtual public space and real public space is that while in both you can efface anonymity if you choose, in real public space you cannot efface reality itself. The only check on increasingly immersive and hence, sophisticated fakes "will hinge on that low-tech practice known as meeting face to face." Lacking a face to face, trust will be reserved. "The legacy of social media will be a world thirsty for new kinds of public experiences."[44]

While Newitz's criticism of the virtual public realm intimates the problem of anonymity leading to incivility, this diagnosis cannot be complete and indeed is mildly self-contradicting. After all, it is entirely possible to be an anonymous person walking across a major city while still feeling constrained not to "flame" passersby—a constriction not enough people apparently feel in digital public space. There is no reason to think that her vision of virtual town halls would improve on this problem. This observation points to the idea that the shortcoming in Habermas's theory lies in its disembodied nature.

Observation of the obvious difference between digital anonymity and urban anonymity owes something to Michel Foucault's insight of the body as the site of discourse. Foucault tells us that the eighteenth century discovered the potential power of the body and began "working it 'retail,' individually; [...] exercising upon it a subtle coercion."[45] Thus, "an art of the human body was born, which was directed not only at the growth of its skills, nor at the intensification of its subjection, but at the formation of a relation that in the mechanism itself makes it more obedient as it becomes more useful."[46] The disciplines over the body gradually improved at the twin objectives of making the body more economically useful while at the same time politically diminished (by, as Marx would elaborate, alienating the individual's laboring body from the complete person). Virtual public space is, by definition, disembodied. Thus, when a crucial function of public space is to provide an outlet for addressing power, in the forms of state power, institutional power, bureaucratic power, corporate power and the like, virtual public space, as recent protestors in Hong Kong have intuited, may be highly useful in a supportive role, but it can never replicate what transpires when bodies assemble. We need to elaborate a philosophy of the relationship between virtual public space and physical public space based on the body to provide a normative guide to both the requirements and the limits of virtual public space as well as its operative relationship with the real thing. The resources that a Foucauldian conception of the body ("theory" may be overstating what Foucault provides) can bring to bolster or to reinforce the many good things about Habermas's public sphere that unfortunately suffer due to his underappreciation of the importance of bodies in urban space as preconditions for communicative rationality.[47]

Think, for example, of what happens when the seemingly interminable ferment on the internet finally does erupt in bodies in urban space in the Occupy Wall Street movement, in Charlottesville, Virginia, or in the Black Lives Matter confrontations. Only at these moments are people taken seriously.

Habermas brushed against this truth in the early 1960s when he granted that "that resistance to discourse must be based on some extra-discursive entity. This entity is the body."[48] But unfortunately the full implications of this observation were not integrated into the basic structure of his conception of the public sphere.

In this book I have argued that architects have yet to fully embrace their potential as a profession because they have yet to embrace a robust concept of the public good that would provide a strong ethical justification for its protected status. In Chapter 1, I provided a number of reasons, from a historical perspective, for this seemingly self-defeating attitude and built toward the idea that an internal clash of values is the root cause undermining the profession. In Chapter 2, I proposed a way to make sense of the profession's embedding in capitalism while explaining why the profit motive, by itself, is insufficient to provide an important public good. I then went on to discuss the new challenges to our profession's core values brought on by globalization. These chapters set the stage for a thorough investigation of the concept of the modern public in Chapter 3, which has its origins in the Enlightenment. Chapter 4 discussed the shifting boundaries between public and private in modern times as analyzed especially by feminist theory. Chapter 5 brought the two chapters on the profession and the two on the public together in a series of proposals for making both architecture and the architecture profession more responsive to the public good. These proposals are surely just a beginning, if the analysis and ideas presented here spark a renewed interest in the potential of the architecture profession as a force for the good. A profession whose members are more unified than they are currently and oriented toward a common ethical purpose will be stronger than the one in which we now practice. When we are a stronger profession, we will be better able to serve the public good and therefore be better able to act on its ideals of a built environment improving all it touches, even as the public realm enters its next transformation.

APPENDIX

Appendix A: Tabulation of Firms

(Featured in *Architectural Record* 1997–2003)

Home state of Firm (1)	Number of Features In Record 1997–2003	Number of resident Architects in state (2)	% Chance of Feature (col 2/ col 3)	State's % of USA registered architects	State's % of total features	% of features/ % of national (col 6/ col 5)
Alabama	1	810	0.1	1%	0.2	0.2
Alaska	0	221	0	0.2%	0	0.0
Arizona	8	1983	0.4	2%	2	1.0
Arkansas	1	450	0.2	0.5%	0.2	0.4
California	108	16,397	0.6	16%	24	1.5
Colorado	2	2869	0.06	3%	0.4	0.16
Connecticut	13	1537	0.8	1.5%	2.9	1.9
Delaware	0	100	0	0.1%	0	0.0
DC	6	770	0.8	1%	1.3	1.3
Florida	5	4551	0.1	4.5%	1.1	0.24
Georgia	7	2406	0.3	2.5%	1.6	0.64
Hawaii	1	922	0.1	1%	0.2	0.2
Idaho	0	481	0	0.5%	0	0.0
Illinois	31	5345	0.6	5%	7	1.4
Indiana	2	955	0.2	1%	0.4	0.4
Iowa	3	442	0.6	0.5%	0.7	1.3
Kansas	3	963	0.3	1%	0.7	0.7
Kentucky	1	657	0.2	0.5%	0.2	0.4
Louisiana	6	1083	0.6	1%	1.4	1.4
Maine	0	375	0	0.5%	0	0.0
Maryland	1	1758	0.05	2%	0.2	0.2
Massachusetts	21	4278	0.5	4%	4.7	1.2
Michigan	2	3564	0.06	3.5%	0.4	0.11
Minnesota	10	1750	0.6	2%	2.2	1.1
Mississippi	1	300	0.3	0.5%	0.2	0.4
Missouri	0	1830	0.0	2%	0.0	0.0

(*continued*)

Home state of Firm (1)	Number of Features In *Record* 1997–2003	Number of resident Architects in state (2)	% Chance of Feature (col 2/ col 3)	State's % of USA registered architects	State's % of total features	% of features/ % of national (col 6/ col 5)
Montana	0	374	0	0.5%	0	0
Nebraska	4	507	0.8	0.5%	0.9	1.8
Nevada	0	522	0	0.5%	0	0
New Hampshire	0	281	0.0	0.2%	0.0	0
New Jersey	2	2895	0.07	3%	0.05	0.17
New Mexico	4	702	0.6	0.5%	0.9	1.8
New York	**140**	**8257**	**1.7**	**8%**	**32.0**	**4 (6)**
North Carolina	7	2003	0.3	2%	1.6	0.8
North Dakota	0	127	0	0.1%	0	0
Ohio	0	3671	0.00	3.5%	0.0	0.00
Oklahoma	4	778	0.5	1%	0.8	0.8
Oregon	8	1063	0.7	1%	1.8	1.8
Pennsylvania	17	3915	0.4	4%	3.8	0.95
Rhode Island	1	243	0.4	2%	0.2	0.1
South Carolina	1	949	0.1	1%	0.2	0.2
South Dakota	0	102	0	0.1%	0	0
Tennessee	3	1369	0.2	1%	0.7	0.7
Texas	5	6803	0.07	7%	1	0.14
Utah	2	689	0.3	0.5%	0.4	0.8
Vermont	1	269	0.3	0.3%	0.2	0.67
Virginia	1	2501	0.03	2.5%	0.2	0.08
Washington	13	3521	0.4	3.5%	2.9	0.83
West Virginia	0	116	0	0.1%	0	0
Wisconsin	0	1612	0	1.6%	0	0
Wyoming	0	110	0	0.1%	0	0
Total	**445**	**101,179**		**101.8% (3)**	**99.7 (4)**	**(5)**

Notes

1. In firms with multiple locations, or with projects attributed to multiple firms, we attempted to attribute the design to the residence state of the acknowledged architect in charge.
2. Source: NCARB's 2004 Survey of Registered Architects.
3. Over 100% due to rounding.
4. Under 100% due to rounding.
5. Geographic representational parity would equal 1. Greater than 1 indicates greater representation in excess of parity, less than 1 indicates underrepresentation. Column 7 allows comparison of relatively likelihood between states, so for example a New York practitioner was 2.2 times more likely to have a feature article than was an Oregon architect (4/ 1.8 = 2.2), 4.2 times as likely as a Pennsylvania architect (4/.95 = 4.2) and 36 times more likely than a Michigan architect (4/ 0.11 = 36). The net geographic winners, in descending order are New York, Connecticut, New Mexico, Oregon, Nebraska, California, Louisiana, DC, Illinois, Massachusetts and Minnesota. All other states just achieved or were below parity.
6. Since all the features garnered by New York architects were drawn from New York City's 3% of the nation's architects, this number would increase from a factor of 4 to a factor of 10.

Appendix B: Top US-based Architecture Firms and Top EA or A Firms:

RANK/ARCHITECTURE FIRM/ $ MIL.

1 GENSLER 175.77
2 SMITHGROUPJJR 57.72
3 STANTEC 44.88
4 ZGF ARCHITECTS LLP 44.80
5 HKS 42.45
6 HMC ARCHITECTS 42.06
7 LPA INC. 41.69
8 SKIDMORE, OWINGS & MERRILL LLP 39.30
9 PERKINS+WILL 36.55
10 HOK 35.56
11 STEINBERG HART 33.86
12 DLR GROUP 32.11
13 LIONAKIS 31.84
14 CARRIER JOHNSON + CULTURE 25.62
15 SOLOMON CORDWELL BUENZ 24.24

(Data source: *ENR*, December 11, 2017 "Top 225 international design firms")
EA or A firms, 2017 revenue in millions from buildings 2016 revenues for the largest International Architecture, AE or EA firms (Data Source *ENR*)

Aecom	2,147
NORR	1443
HDR	1,388
DAR Group	1,114
Gensler	1,088
Jacobs	895
Sweco AB	675
WS Atkins	620
Stantec	605
China State Construction Engineering	600
Arcplus group	500
HOK	400
HKS	390
Burns and McDonnell	333
Skidmore Owings Merrill	326
IBI Group	234
Thornton Tomasetti	230
Khatib & Alami	225
Perkins Eastman	214

Cannondesign	191
Populous	186
NBBJ	164
AEDAS	155
Woods Bagot	146
ZGF	142
Kohn Pederson Fox	133
Page Southerland Page	131
Proger SPa	120
NKY Architects	120
BEGA Group	106
KEO Intl	105
Day & Zimmerman	105
CDI Corp	92
China Aluminum	92
EHAF consulting Engineers	81
ECG Engineering	75
Studios Architecture	72
Arquitectonica	70
Cunningham Group Architecture	69
Merrick & Co.	69
Heerim Architects and Planners	69
SSH	68
Robert A. M. Stern	68
WATG + Wimberly	67
Sasaki	60
Morrison Hershfield	56
Dewan Architects and Engineers	51
Assoc. Consulting Engineers	50
Architecture and Planning Group	49
MG2	47
Tecnica Y Proyectos	45
Wong Tung and Partners	41
Stanley consultants	41
Smith & Gill	26
Goettsch Partners	26
Rebel Design Group	26
IDOM	25
Arabtech Jardaneh	24
Samoo	24
AMG Al Amar	20
KCCT	20
Dar Al Omran	19
ZAS Architects	18
Shangdong de Jian Group	11
Consolidated Consultants Group	11
Distance Studio	10
Salfo & Assocs	5

NOTES

Chapter 1 The Architecture Profession and the Public Good

1. Staff, "AIANY Issues Statement Against Designing Spaces of Incarceration Within the Current U.S. Justice System," *Architect*, September 30, 2020. Oliver Wainwright, "Architecture Furlough Fraud, Snooping and Firings: Architects Speak Out over Lockdown Exploitation," *The Guardian*, October 12, 2020.
2. For those unfamiliar with their exploits,

   When Louis Kahn died of a heart attack in Pennsylvania Station in 1974, he left a legacy of a handful of great buildings, 3 neglected families (two of which were secret) and a personal debt approaching half a million dollars despite the fact that his employees often went unpaid. This story is told in *Nathaniel Kahn, My Architect, A Son's Journey.* HBO/Cinemax Films, 2003, and elsewhere.

   After leaving his wife and 8 children to run off to Europe with the wife of a client, Frank Lloyd Wright subsidized his lifestyle for decades on the unpaid labor of the students of his school. This story is told in Brendan Gill, *The Many Masks of Frank Lloyd Wright* (New York: Putnam, 1987) and elsewhere.

   Mies, thinking that art lay above politics, sought the favor of Hitler only to abandon his wife to the Nazis and move to America when it became evident that Nazis didn't like modernism. This story is told in Elaine S. Hochman, *Architects of Fortune: Mies Van Der Rohe and the Third Reich* (New York: Grove Press, 1989).

   About Richard Meier, more in Chapter 4.
3. David Watkin, *George III and the Culture of the Enlightenment*. Royal Collection Publications, London, 2004. Frontispiece.
4. Benjamin Pauker, "Frank Gehry," *Foreign Policy*, 201 (July/August 2013): 24. Renier de Graaf, *Four Walls and a Roof: The Complex Nature of a Simple Profession* (Cambridge, MA: Harvard University Press, 2017), 324.
5. Denise Scott Brown, "Room at the Top? Sexism and the Star System in Architecture," in *Architecture: A Place for Women*, ed. Ellen Berkeley (Washington, DC: Smithsonian Institution Press, 1989), 237–46 (241).
6. Thomas Fisher, "Making the Case for Higher Fees," *Architect*, March 12, 2014, https://www.architectmagazine.com/practice/best-practices/making-the-case-for-higher-fees_o (accessed on November 20, 2020).
7. Ibid.
8. Jean-Paul Carlhian, "The Ecole des Beaux-Arts: Modes and Manners," *Journal of Architectural Education*, 33 (November 1979): 7–17 (17).

9. John Mead Howells, "A French Government School from the Inside," *Century Illustrated Monthly Magazine*, 62 (1901): 860–68 (861). See also Howells's article, *The École des Beaux-Arts* (New York: Architectural Record Company, 1901) (emphasis added).
10. Ibid., 862.
11. Ibid., 863.
12. Elaine Hochman, *Bauhaus: Crucible of Modernism* (New York: Fromm International, 1997) 82–83.
13. Ibid., 141.
14. Thomas Hacker, in an interview with J. M. Cava, "Our Architect: Working with Louis Kahn," *Arcade*, posted on January 26, 2016.
15. Scott Brown, "Room at the Top?" 241.
16. Howells, "A French Government School from the Inside," 862.
17. Stella Lee, "Where Is Architecture's #MeToo Moment?" *New York Times*, October 12, 2018.
18. Andrew Maynard, "Work/Life/Work Balance," https://www.archdaily.com/234633/work-life-work-balance-by-andrew-maynard, August, 2018.
19. Roxanne Kuter Williamson, *American Architects and the Mechanics of Fame*. (Austin: University of Texas Press, 1991), 6.
20. Ibid., 230. See also, Garry Stevens, *The Favored Circle* (Cambridge, MA: MIT Press, 1998).
21. Lee, "Where Is Architecture's #MeToo Moment?".
22. A. de Graft-Johnson, S. Manley, and C. Greed, *Why Do Women Leave Architecture?* London: RIBA. www.architecture.com/Files/RIBAProfessionalServices/Education/DiscussionPapers/WhyDoWomenLeaveArchitecture, (2003), (accessed on April 2008) and S. Manley, and the follow-up paper by A. de Graft-Johnson, "Women in Architecture: Five Years On," edited by A. Dainty, Procs *24th Annual ARCOM Conference, 1-3 September 2008* (Cardiff, UK: Association of Researchers in Construction Management), 891–900.
23. Ernest L. Boyer and Lee D. Mitgang, *Building Community: A New Future for Architectural Education and Practice* (Princeton, NJ: Carnegie Foundation for the Advancement of Teaching, 1996), 133.
24. Ibid., 136.
25. Ibid., 145.
26. Ibid., 145.
27. Ibid., 147.
28. https://www.dol.gov/whd/regs/compliance/hrg.htm.
29. Katherine Keane, "AIA: Licensing Protects the Public," *Architect* , January 25, 2018 https://www.architectmagazine.com/practice/aia-licensing-protects-the-public_o.
30. Steven Bingler and Martin C. Peterson, "How to Rebuild Architecture," *New York Times*, December 15, 2014.
31. Aaron Betsky, "*The New York Times* Versus Architecture," *Architect*, December 23, 2014.
32. Ibid.
33. Ibid.
34. Justin Shubow, "Architecture Continues to Implode: More Insiders Admit the Profession Is Failing," *Forbes*, January 6, 2015, (accessed on November 20, 2020)
35. Architects Registration Board. *Architects Code: Standards of Conduct and Practice.* London: Architects Registration Board, http://www.arb.org.uk/wp-content/uploads/2016/05/Architects-Code-2017.pdf . Royal Institute of British Architects. *Code of Professional*

Conduct, London: RIBA. https://www.architecture.com/knowledge-and-resources/resources-landing-page/code-of-professional-conduct#:~:text=Honesty%2C%20integrity%20and%20competence%2C%20as,effect%20on%201%20May%202019. American Institute of Architects, *Code of Ethics and Professional Conduct*, https://www.aia.org/pages/3296-code-of-ethics-and-professional-conduct

36 National Society of Professional Engineers. *2003 Code of Ethics* (Alexandria, VA: NSPE), 2003. American Medical Association, *Code of Medical Ethics*, https://www.ama-assn.org/delivering-care/ethics/code-medical-ethics-overview.
Simon Foxell, *Professionalism for the Built Environment* (London: Routledge, 2018), 222.

37 When the designers of a code of ethics do not actually have to think about how the document may function as a guide for enforcement, they can produce something considerably more comprehensive, as here with The Ethical Code of the Architects' Council of Europe (ACE):

> All providers of architectural services must respect and help to conserve and develop the system of values and the natural and cultural heritage of the community in which they are creating architecture. They shall strive not only to improve the environment through the highest quality of design but also to improve the quality of the life and the habitat within such a community in a sustainable manner, particularly considering energy and water conservation and reducing carbon emissions in the context of world climate change, being fully mindful of the effect of their work on the widest interests of all those who may reasonably be expected to use or enjoy the product of their work. (ACE, [2], Principle 2.1)

38 Jeremy Till, *Architecture Depends* (Cambridge MA: MIT Press, 2013), 180.
39 https://www.architecture.com/knowledge-and-resources/resources-landing-page/code-of-professional-conduct#:~:text=Honesty%2C%20integrity%20and%20competence%2C%20as,effect%20on%201%20May%202019.
40 Paul Morrell, "Collaboration for Change: The Edge Commission Report on the Future of Professionalism," https://edgedebate.com/blog/collaboration-for-change-amp-the-core-cities. (accessed on November 1, 2020).

Chapter 2 The Architecture Profession in Capitalism

1 Douglas E. Hough and Charles G. Kratz, "Can 'Good' Architecture Meet the Market Test?" *Journal of Urban Economics*, 14:1 (1983): 40–54, 50.
2 Ibid., 51.
3 Judith Blau, *Architects and Firms* (Cambridge, MA: MIT Press, 1987), 114.
4 Kerry D. Vandell and Jonathan S. Lane, "The Economics of Architecture and Urban Design: Some Preliminary Findings," *AREUEA: Journal of the American Real Estate & Urban Economics Association*, 17:2 (Summer 1989): 235–60, 257.
5 Kerry Vandell, "Economics of Office Design," *ULI Research Working Paper Series*, paper 603 (Washington, DC: Urban Land Institute, July 1992).
6 John E. Czarnecki, "Expressing the Art of Good Business," *Architectural Record*, 89:10 (October 2001): 90–108. Clifford A. Pearson, "Making Good Design Pay Off," *Architectural Record*, (October 2000): 84–106. James S. Russell, "Good Design is Good Business: Second Annual Business Week/Architectural Record Awards," *Architectural Record*, 186:10 (October 1998): 88–102. James S. Russell, "Taking the Measure of

Design and the Bottom Line, "*Architectural Record*, 187:10 (October 999): 84–104. Karen D. Stein, "Good Design is Good Business," *Architectural Record*, 185: 10 (October 1997): 54–64.

7   Thomas Piketty, *Capital in the Twenty-First Century*, trans. Arthur Goldhammer (Cambridge, MA: Belknap Press, 2014).
8   Congressional Budget Office, "Trends in the distribution of Household Income Between 1979 and 2007," https://www.cbo.gov/publication/42729 (accessed on November 11, 2020).
9   https://www.aecom.com/content/wp-content/uploads/2018/01/AECOM-Press-Fact-Sheet.pdf.
10 Anonymous, "How Midsize Engineering and Architectural Firms Prosper" *Engineering News-Record*, May 4, 2015.
11 American Institute of Architects, 2018 Firm Survey Report (Washington, DC: The American Institute of Architects, 2019). http://content.aia.org/sites/default/files/2018-08/2018-AIA-Firm-Survey-Overview.pdf.
12 IHS Economics: Construction Global Outlook, 2013. https://ihsmarkit.com/pdf/IHS_Global_Construction_ExecSummary_Feb2014_1408521109130 52132.pdf.
13 Elizabeth Evitts Dickinson, "The Fifty-Year-Old Intern Architect," *Architect*, October 7, 2011. https://www.architectmagazine.com/design/the-50-year-old-intern-architect_o.
14 James R. Faulconbridge and Daniel Muzio, "Professions in a Globalizing World: Towards a Transnational Sociology of the Professions," *International Sociology*, 26:6 (November 18, 2011): 136–52, 143.
15 Michael Zimmerman, "Globalization, Multiculturalism, and Architectural Ethics," *Architecture, Ethics and Globalization*, ed. Graham Owen (New York: Routledge, 2009), 158–70.
16 Thomas Fisher, *Ethics for Architects: Fifty Dilemmas of Professional Practice* (Hudson, NY: Princeton Architectural Press, 2010), 9.
17 Martin Filler, "The Insolence of Architecture," *New York Review of Books*, June 5, 2014. Also see Hanna Kozlowska, "When Buildings Are Political, Should Architects Be Politicians?" *New York Times*, September 2, 2014.
18 Rory Olcayto, "Take an Ethical Stance, Libeskind Tells his Peers," *Building Design*, February 15, 2008, 3.
19 Farid Abdel-Nour, "Liberalism and Ethnocentrism," *Journal of Political Philosophy*, 8:2 (2000): 207–26, 211.
20 Richard Rorty, *Objectivity, Relativism and Truth: Philosophical Papers*, volume 1, (Cambridge: Cambridge University Press, 1990), 31 footnote 13.
21 Bryan Fanning and Timothy Mooney, "Pragmatism and Intolerance: Nietzsche and Rorty," *Philosophy and Social Criticism*, 36:6 (June 25, 2010): 735–55, 742.
22 Ibid., 743.
23 Richard Rorty. *Truth and Progress: Philosophical Papers*, volume 3 (Cambridge: Cambridge University Press, 1993), 178.
24 Abdel-Nour, "Liberalism and Ethnocentrism," 225.
25 Abdel-Nour, "Liberalism and Ethnocentrism," 216.
26 James Riach, "Zaha Hadid Defends World Cup Role Following Migrant Worker Deaths," *The Guardian*, February 25, 2014.
27 Edwin Heathcote, "Starchitects Risk Losing Lustre," *Financial Times*, September 8, 2011.
28 Rorty, *Objectivity, Relativism and Truth*, 203.

29 Amartya Sen, "The Global Reach of Human Rights," *Journal of Applied Philosophy*, 29:2 (2012): 91–100 (100).
30 Richard Rorty, "What's Wrong with 'Rights'," *Harper's Magazine*, June 1996, 15–18,15. Also at: https://www.thefreelibrary.com/What%27s+wrong+with+%22rights.%22(excerpt+from+a+speech+by+Richard...-a018311735.
31 Amartya Sen, *Development as Freedom* (New York: Anchor Books, 1999), 151.

Chapter 3 Who Is the Public?

1   Curtis Fentress, *Public Architecture: The Art Inside* (San Francisco: Oro Editions, 2011); Curtis Fentress, *Touchstones of Design: ReDefining Public Architecture* (Mulgrave, AU: Images Publishing, 2010); Jan Gehl, *Life between Buildings: Using Public Space* (Washington, DC: Island Press, 2011); Jan Gehl and Birgitte Svarre, *How to Study Public Life* (Washington, DC: Island Press, 2013)
2   Numa Denis Fustel de Coulanges. *The Ancient City* (Gloucester, MA: Peter Smith, 1979, [1864]), 221.
3   Diedre A. McCloskey, *Bourgeois Equality: How Ideas, Not Capital or Institutions, Enriched the World* (Chicago: University of Chicago Press, 2016), xv.
4   Ibid.
5   K. M. Macdonald, *The Sociology of the Professions* (London: Sage, 1995), 39.
6   McCloskey, *Bourgeois Equality*, xv.
7   Peter Boettke and Rosolino Candela, "Comparative Historical Political Economy and the Bourgeois Era," *Journal of Private Enterprise*, 32:4 (2017): 27.
8   Immanuel Kant, "What Is Enlightenment?" written in 1784, first published in 1798 in the *Berlin Monthly*. Marxists.org/reference/subject/ethics/kant/enlightenment.htm.
9   Denis Diderot, *Les Bijoux Indiscrets* (Project Gutenberg: https://www.gutenberg.org/files/54672/54672-h/54672-h.htm#CHAP_XXIX) Chapter XXIX.
10 Boettke and Candela, "Comparative Historical Political Economy," 28.
11 Scott Taylor, "Book Review," *Organizational Studies*, 38:I (2017): 152.
12 David Boaz, "Opinion: Bourgeois Virtues," *The Guardian*, July 14, 2006.
13 As quoted by Stewart Sutherland, "Scottish Enlightenment," https://www.britannica.com/event/Scottish-Enlightenment. Also in Encyclopaedia *Britannica: The Ideas That Made the Modern World* (Britannica Guides Series) The People, Philosophy and History of the Enlightenment, 2008, 15.
14 Sutherland, "Scottish Enlightenment," 15.
15 *Encyclopaedia Britannica: The Ideas That Made the Modern World* (Britannica Guides Series) The People, Philosophy and History of the Enlightenment, 2008, 153.
16 Charles Taylor, *Philosophical Arguments* (Cambridge, MA: Harvard University Press, 1995), 262.
17 Ibid., 265.
18 Ibid.
19 Alexis de Tocqueville, *The Old Regime and the Revolution*, trans. John Bonner (New York: Harper & Brothers, 1856), 172–73.
20 Taylor, *Philosophical Arguments*, 259.
21 Macdonald, *The Sociology of the Professions*, 72.
22 Boettke and Candela, "Comparative Historical Political Economy," 25.
23 Karl Marx and Friedrich Engels, *The Communist Manifesto*, https://www.marxists.org/archive/marx/works/1848/communist-manifesto/ch01.htm.

24 Jürgen Habermas, *The Structural Transformation of the Public Sphere: An Inquiry into a Category of Bourgeois Society* (Cambridge, MA: MIT Press, 1991), 4.
25 Ibid., 87.
26 Ibid., 88.
27 Michael E. Gardiner, "Wild Publics and Grotesque Symposiums: Habermas and Bakhtin on Dialogue, Everyday Life and the Public Sphere," in *After Habermas: New Perspectives on the Public Sphere*, ed. Nick Crossley and John Michael Roberts (New York: Wiley-Blackwell, 2004), 43.
28 Habermas, *The Structural Transformation of the Public Sphere*, 88 (emphasis in the original).
29 Ibid.
30 Ibid.
31 Michael J. Sandel, *Democracy's Discontent: America in Search of a Public Philosophy* (Cambridge MA: Harvard University Press, 1996), 26.
32 Margaret Thatcher, interviewed in *Woman's Own*, September 23, 1987. The full interview can be found online at: https://www.margaretthatcher.org/document/106689.
33 Robert Kuttner, *Everything for Sale: The Virtues and Limits of Markets* (Chicago: University of Chicago Press, 1996), 333.
34 Robert Putnam. *Bowling Alone: The Collapse and Revival of American Community* (New York: Simon and Schuster, 2000).
35 Martin Pawley, *The Private Future: Causes and Consequences of Community Collapse in the West* (London: Thames and Hudson, 1973), 179.
36 Stuart Hampshire, "Morality and Pessimism," *Public and Private Morality* (Cambridge: Cambridge University Press, 1978), 2.
37 Joseph B. Pine and James H. Gilmore, *The Experience Economy* (Cambridge, MA: Harvard Business Press, 1999),
38 Michael Benedikt, "Reality and Authenticity in the Experience Economy," *Architectural Record*, 189:11 (2001): 84–87, 85.
39 Kuttner, *Everything for Sale*, 338.
40 Alasdair MacIntyre, *After Virtue: A Study in Moral Theory* (South Bend, IN: Notre Dame University Press, 1981).
41 Ibid.
42 Michael Warner, *Publics and Counterpublics* (New York: Zone Books, 2005), 56–57.
43 https://www.noma.net/noma-presidents-desk/.
44 https://www.insightintodiversity.com/growth-in-racial-diversity-among-architects-is-slow-but-experts-say-the-conversation-continues/. The *Directory of African American Architects* reports 470 living black female architects and 1836 black male architects in 2019
45 Victoria Kaplan, *Structural Inequality: Black Architects in the United States* (New York: Rowman and Littlefield, 2006), 3.
46 https://www.noma.net/wp-content/uploads/2020/10/NOMA-Magazine-FALL-2020_vFinal_spreads2.pdf. For those interested in further reading about Habermas, two excellent collections of essays not referenced here are:

> Craig Calhoun, ed. *Habermas and the Public Sphere* (Cambridge, MA: MIT Press, 1992). Stephen K. White, ed. *The Cambridge Companion to Habermas* (Cambridge, UK: Cambridge University Press), 1995.

Chapter 4 Public and Private

1. Nancy Fraser, "Rethinking the Public Sphere: A Contribution to the Critique of Actually Existing Democracy," *Social Text* 25:26 (1990): 56–80 (67).
2. Virginia Held flatly states: "Feminists reject the implication that what occurs in the household occurs as if on an island beyond politics. In fact, the personal is highly affected by the political power beyond [...]" in *Feminist Morality: Transforming Culture, Society, and Politics* (Chicago: University of Chicago Press, 1993), 54.
3. Ibid., 127.
4. Margaret Urban Walker, "Moral Understandings: Alternative 'Epistemology' for a Feminist Ethics" In *Explorations in Feminist Ethics*, ed. Eve Browning Cole and Susan Coultrap-McQuin (Bloomington: University of Indiana Press, 1992), 166.
5. Joan Tronto, *Moral Boundaries: A Political Argument for an Ethic of Care* (New York: Routledge, 1994), 57.
6. Moira Gatens, *Feminism and Philosophy: Perspectives on Difference and Equality* (Bloomington, IN: Polity Press, 1991), 85.
7. Ibid.
8. Tronto, *Moral Boundaries*, 96.
9. Beatriz Colomina, "Battle Lines: E.1027," in *The Architect: Reconstructing Her Practice*, ed. Francesca Hughes (Cambridge MA: MIT Press, 1996), 9.
10. Caroline Fraser, "When Will We Care About Domestic Violence?" *New York Review of Books* (May 28, 2020): 14–16, 16.
11. Tronto, *Moral Boundaries*, 169.
12. Ibid., 106–8, 115.
13. Ibid., 105.
14. Ibid., 103.
15. Brenda Vale, "Gender and an Architecture of Environmental Responsibility," in *Desiring Practices: Architecture, Gender and the Interdisciplinary*, ed. Duncan McCorquodale, Katerina Rüedi, and Sarah Wigglesworth (London: Black Dog, 1996), 272.
16. Tronto, *Moral Boundaries*, 104 (emphasis added).
17. It should be noted, however, that a small but persistently dissenting voice in moral philosophy places great weight on the value of art. Iris Murdoch, for example, asserts that art provides lessons in virtue. Great art, she writes, is "where virtue really shines." "The Sovereignty of Good over other Concepts" in *Virtue Ethics*, ed. Roger Crisp and Michael Slote (Oxford: Oxford University Press, 1997), 115. Toward healing this opposition between ethics and aesthetics Alisdair MacIntyre indicates a different, and given this discussion, highly relevant way of distinguishing between moral and non-moral activities. In "The Nature of the Virtues" he distinguishes between activities that are not social practices such as throwing a football well, planting turnips, and bricklaying, and those that are, such as farming and architecture. This is an important distinction because it is only out of such practices that the "concept of virtue becomes clear." *Virtue Ethics*, 124. But these dissenters are the exception rather than the norm in moral philosophy.
18. Fraser, "Rethinking the Public Sphere," 73.
19. George Chauncy, "Privacy Could Only Be Had in Public: Gay Uses of the Streets," *Stud: Architectures of Masculinity*, ed. Joel Sanders (New York: Princeton Architectural Press, 1996), 224–68.

20 Aaron Betsky, *Queer Space: Architecture and Same Sex Desire* (New York: William Morrow, 1997). Betsky asserts that one aspect of queer space is that it seeks less to provide a domination over the built environment than a mirroring of the self in it. But other assertions, such as that queer space is theatrical are hard to separate from the grossest stereotypes. He suggests that the display and elaboration of queer space coincides with the rediscovery of the body in general. During early Christianity, for example, when the flesh was considered foul, the queer space of public baths disappeared. Another aspect of queer space: it fights the normalizing tendencies of mainstream built environments. Betsky argues that the influence of women and men differs in the construction of public queer spaces. Gay men tend to be more territorial and possibly ghetto-ized and isolated than do lesbians. Thus undermining the construction of the gender argument all over again, by asserting a gender difference even among groups where gender roles are almost entirely constructed rather than assumed: "Lesbian communities have tended to be stronger, longer-lasting, and less exclusive, so that they point the way toward the making of a realized social sphere that does not repeat the ghettolike isolation in which gay men have found themselves." (176). Betsky's pursuit of queer spaces ultimately liberates them from being concerned exclusively with gender and becomes instead more about humans opposing the normalizing role of the construction of space, which gives preference to certain activities and discourages others. But this very liberating of "queer" from sexual boundary undermines the very idea that the construction of gender plays a determining role in establishing the domains of public and private. Instead, it appears that more universal human needs—to resist prejudice and stereotype, to make a meaningful place in the world, to take care of unaddressed needs—do far more to determine the built environment.
21 Jacob Ward, "Won't You Be My Neighbor?" *Architecture*, 91:4 (April 2002): 72.
22 Kim Tanzer and Caroline Constant, "Center for Women's Studies and Gender Research, University of Florida, 1994–2000," *Journal of Architectural Education*, 55:2 (November 2001): 81–89.
23 (https://www.fastcompany.com/90164300/exclusive-why-i-started-a-shitty-architecture-men-list (accessed, October 2018).
24 http://content.aia.org/sites/default/files/2020-05/2020_Code_of_Ethics.pdf.
25 Despina Stratigakos, *Where Are the Women Architects?* (Princeton: Princeton University Press, 2016), 34.
26 Ibid., 28.
27 Ann de Graft-Johnson, Sandra Manley, and Clara Greed, *Why Do Women Leave Architecture?* Bristol, UK: RIBA and the University of West England, 2003. www.architecture.com/Files/RIBAProfessionalServices/Education/ DiscussionPapers/WhyDoWomenLeaveArchitecture (accessed on April 2008).
28 David Brusset, "Still Allowed to Like Meier?" https://architecturehereandthere.com/2018/03/14/still-allowed-to-like-meier/.
29 Aaron Betsky, "Waiting to Be Weinsteined: When Will Accusations of Sexual Harassment Arise in Architecture?" *Architect*, November 21, 2017. Architectmagazine.com/practice/waiting-to-be-weinsteined-when-will-accusations-of-sexual-harassment-arise-in-architecture_o (accessed on November 20, 2020).
30 For example: Thomas Hinchcliffe's discussion of French courtesans as architectural clients, Helen Hill's discussion of Italian Convents, and Louise Durning's discussion of Lady Margaret Beaufort in Louise Durning and Mark Wrigley, eds. *Gender and Architecture* (New York: John Wiley, 2000). Vanessa Chase, "Edith Wharton,

The Decoration of Houses, and Gender in Turn-of-the-Century America," in *Architecture and Feminism*, ed. Debra Coleman, Elizabeth Danze, and Carol Handerson (New York: Princeton Architectural Press, 1996), 130–60. Susan R. Henderson, "A Revolution in the Woman's Sphere: Grete Lihotzky and the Frankfurt Kitchen," in *Architecture and Feminism*, ed. Debra Coleman, Elizabeth Danze, and Carol Handerson, (New York: Princeton Architectural Press, 1996), 221–53. Meaghan Morris, "Great Moments in Social Climbing: King Kong and the Human Fly," in *Sexuality and Space*, ed. Beatriz Colomina (New York: Princeton Architectural Press, 1992), 1–52.

31 For example, Leslie Kanes Weisman, *Discrimination by Design* (Urbana: University of Illinois Press, 1992).

Sharon Sutton, "Resisting the Patriarchal Norms of Professional Education," in *The Sex of Architecture*, Diana Agrest, Patricia Conway, and Leslie Kanes Weisman (New York: Abrams, 1996), 287–94.

32 For example, Mary McLeod, "Other Spaces and Others," in *The Sex of Architecture*, Diana Agrest, Patricia Conway, and Leslie Kanes Weisman (New York: Harry Abrams, 1996), 15–28. Catherine Ingraham "Losing it in Architecture," in *The Architect: Reconstructing Her Practice*, ed. Francesca Hughes (Cambridge, MA: MIT Press, 1996), 148–63.

33 Jennifer Bloomer, "The Matter of the Cutting Edge," in *Desiring Practices: Architecture, Gender and the Interdisciplinary*, ed. Duncan McCorquodale,, Katerina Rüedi, and Sarah Wigglesworth (London: Black Dog, 1996), 11–31 (20).

34 For example: Merrill Elam, "Projects/ Recollections," in *The Architect: Reconstructing Her Practice*, ed. Francesca Hughes (Cambridge, MA: MIT Press, 1996), 182–99. Richter, Dagmar, "A Practice of One's Own: The Critical Copy and Translarion of Space," in *The Architect: Reconstructing Her Practice*, ed. Francesca Hughes (Cambridge, MA: MIT Press, 1996), 96–127. Denise Scott Brown, "Through the Looking Glass," in, *The Sex of Architecture*, ed. Diana Agrest, et. al. (New York: Abrams Publishers, 1996), 211–16.

35 Lori A. Brown, *Contested Spaces: Abortion Clinics, Women's Shelters and Hospitals* (London: Taylor & Francis, 2013), 24.

36 Homi K. Bhabha in "Our Neighbors, Ourselves: Contemporary Reflections on Survival," (Hegel Lectures Series, https://doi.org/10.1515/9783110262445, 2011, 6) called it "an interstitial realm of the in-between—a space and time of 'thirdness.'" The concept of the "Third Space" has been employed, for example, in Celia Whitechurch, "Shifting Identities and Blurring Boundaries: The Emergence of *Third Space* Professionals in UK Higher Education," *Higher Education Quarterly*, 62:4 (2008): 377–96. And in Linda McDowell's essay "Spatializing Feminism," in *Bodyspace: Destabilizing Geographies of Gender and Sexuality*, ed. Nancy Duncan (London: Routledge, 1996), 27–46.

37 Jane Rendell's essay "Only Resist: A Feminist Approach to Critical Spatial Practice," *Architecture Review* (February 19, 2018), https://www.architectural-review.com/essays/only-resist-a-feminist-approach-to-critical-spatial-practice (accessed on November 20, 2020), relays that after a relatively quiet first millennial decade, the decade beginning in 2010 has been an active time for feminist architecture to explore its more reflective, performative, intersectional, and material aspects. A renewed interest in interior design by feminist architects may portend a more active exploration of the public/private divide.

38 Mary L. Morrison, ed., *Historic Savannah: Survey of Significant Buildings in the Historic and Victorian Districts of Savannah, Georgia* (Savannah: Historic Savannah Foundation and The Junior League of Savannah, 1979), vi–vii.

Chapter 5 Toward an Architecture of Publicness

1 Sarah Whiting quoted in "Architecture and Dispersal," ed. Rafi Segal and Els Verbakel, discussion with Stan Allen, Marcel Smets, Sarah Whiting and Margaret Crawford, *Architectural Design*, 78:1 (January/February 2008): (102–7), 103.
2 Ibid., 106.
3 Dana Villa, "Postmodernism and the Public Sphere," *American Political Science Review*, 86:3 (1992): 712–21, 719.
4 Margaret Crawford, "Contesting the Public Realm: Struggles Over Public Space in Los Angeles," *Journal of Architectural Education*, 49:1 (1995–96): 4–9, 4.
5 Some notable exceptions: Aldo van Eyck's playgrounds, Alvar Aalto's public works.
6 "Architecture and Dispersal," 106.
7 Dana Cuff, "Collective Form: The Status of Public Architecture," *Thresholds*, 40 (2012): 55–66, 62. Cuff will allow the following: "Of course there are still city halls, parks, courthouses, libraries and schools, and these continue to materially render what we share. Today, these buildings are portraits of efficiency and utility, dressed in an aesthetic that could be called 'thriftwashing,' a thin coat of architecture that expresses a priority on economizing, whether or not the building is actually cost-effective."
8 Cathleen McGuigan, "Architecture and the Future of the Public Realm," *Architectural Record*, April 1, 2017. Architecturalrecord.com/articles/12452-architecture-and-the-future-of-the-public-realm
9 Ibid.
10 Karrie Jacobs, "Public Space in the Trump Era," *Architect*, (3/2017): 74–80, 74.
11 Winnie Hu, "Hostile Architecture: How Public Spaces Keep the Public Out," *New York Times,* November 8, 2019. and Winnie Hu, "Times Insider: How We Searched for Hostile Architecture in New York," *New York Times*, November 8, 2019.
12 Stephen Schmidt, Jeremy Nemeth, and Erik Botsford, "The Evolution of Privately Owned Public Spaces in New York City," *Urban Design International*, 16:4 (Winter, 2011): 270–84, 276.
13 Jeremy Nemeth and Stephen Schmidt, "The Privatization of Public Space: Modeling and Measuring Publicness," *Environment and Planning B: Planning and Design*, 38 (2011): 5–23, 9.
14 Hu, "Hostile Architecture."
15 Jeremy Németh, "Defining a Public: The Management of Privately Owned Public Space," *Urban Studies*, 46:11 (October, 2009): 2463–90, 2478.
16 Te-Sheng Huang and Karen A. Franck, "Let's Meet at Citicorp: Can Privately Owned Public Spaces be Inclusive?" *Journal of Urban Design*, 23:4 (August 2018): 499–517, 499.
17 Ibid., 516.
18 Michael Benedikt, "Reality and Authenticity in the Experience Economy," *Architectural Record*, 189:11 (2001): 84–87, 85.
19 John Dewey, *Art as Experience* (New York: Capricorn Books, 1934), 4.
20 Michael J. Sandel, *Democracy's Discontent: America in Search of a Public Philosophy* (Cambridge, MA: Harvard University Press, 1996).

21 Ibid.
22 Sylvia Lavin, "CRITICISM: One Person at a Time," *Architectural Record*, 195:8 (August 2007): 106–17.
23 Sylvia Lavin, "Re-Reading the Encyclopedia: Architectural Theory and the Formation of the Public in Late Eighteenth-Century France," *Journal of the Society of Architectural Historians*, 53:2 (1994): 184–92, 192.
24 Diane Viegut Al Shihabi, "Caractére Types and the Beaux-Arts Tradition: Interpreting Academic Typologies of Form and Decorum," *Athens Journal of Architecture*, 3:3 (July 2017): 227–50, 230.
25 J. J. P. Oud, "Art and Machine," *De Stijl*, 1:3 (1918): 25–27. The Shell Building in The Hague (1938–1942) was part of Oud's response to what he perceived as the International Style's crisis of monumentality.
26 For a fuller discussion, see Nicholas Ray, "Bibliotecas nacionales en la ciudad europea del siglo veinte: Londres y Paris" in *Biblioteca, Ciudad y Sociedad: Plan Maestro Biblioteca Nacional de Chile*, 74–91. Biblioteca Nacional de Chile *ISBN 978-956-244-304-3*.
27 Samuel Scheffler, *The Afterlife*, The Tanner Lectures on Human Values, Berkeley: University of California, March 13–15, 2012, 175.
28 Ibid., 179.
29 Dale Jamieson, *Reason in a Dark Time: Why the Struggle Against Climate Change Failed—and What It Means for Our Future* (New York: Oxford University Press, 2014), 104.
30 Ibid., 144.
31 Stephen Gardiner, "A Perfect Moral Storm: Climate Change Intergenerational Ethics and the Problem of Moral Corruption," *Environmental Values*, 15:3 (2006): 397–413.
32 Clive Hamilton, "Moral Collapse in a Warming World," *Ethics and International Affairs*, 28:3 (2014): 335–42, 341.
33 Matthew Coffay, "The Intergenerational Ethics of Climate Change," (dissertation) University of Bergen, Department of Philosophy, 2019, 19.
34 Douglas MacLean and Peter G. Brown, eds. *Energy and the Future* (Totowa, NJ: Rowman and Littlefield, 1983), 166–79.
35 Susanne Tauber, Martijn van Zomeren, and Maja Kutlaca, "Should the Moral Core of Climate Issues be Emphasized or Downplayed in Public Discourse?" *Climatic Change*, 130:3 (2015): 453–64, 457.
36 Stephen Gardiner, S. Caney, D. Jamieson, and H. Shue, eds., *Climate Ethics: Essential Readings* (Oxford: Oxford University Press, 2010), 118.
37 Kathryn B. Janda and Yael Parag, "A Middle-Out Approach for Improving Energy Performance in Buildings," *Building Research & Information*, 41:1 (2013): 39–50.
38 Malcolm Bull, "What Is the Rational Response?" *London Review of Books*, 34:10 (May 2012), Lrb.co.uk/the-paper/v34/n10/malcolmbull/what-is-the-rational-response (accessed on November 20, 2020).
39 Will Hughes and Cathy Hughes, "Professionalism and Professional Institutions in Times of Change" *Building Research & Information*, 41:1 (2013): 28.
40 Robert Kuttner, "Blaming Liberalism," *New York Review of Books*, (November 21, 2019): (36–38), 38.
41 Evan Stewart and Douglas Hartmann, "The New Structural Transformation of the Public Sphere," *Sociological Theory*, 38:2 (June 4, 2020): 170–91.
42 Annalee Newitz, "A Better Social Media World Is Waiting for Us," *New York Times*, November 30, 2019.
43 Ibid.

44 Ibid.
45 Michel Foucault, *Discipline and Punish*, trans. Alan Sheridan, 2nd ed. (New York: Vintage Books, 1995), 137.
46 Ibid., 137–38.
47 Daniel Punday, "Foucault's Body Tropes," *New Literary History*, 31 (2000): 509–28, 509. "The widespread popularity of Foucault's description of the body as a site of power, even among those critics who question the value of Foucault's theory in general, suggests that it performs a function within critical analysis that is somewhat independent of Foucault's theory."
48 Ibid., 521.

BIBLIOGRAPHY

Abdel-Nour, Farid. "Liberalism and Ethnocentrism," *Journal of Political Philosophy*, 8:2 (2000): 207–26.

AECOM Press Fact Sheet, https://www.aecom.com/content/wp-content/uploads/2018/01/AECOM-Press-Fact-Sheet.pdf (accessed on November 1, 2020).

Al Shihabi, Diane Viegut. "Caractére Types and the Beaux-Arts Tradition: Interpreting Academic Typologies of Form and Decorum," *Athens Journal of Architecture*, 3:3 (July 2017): 227–50.

American Institute of Architects, *Code of Ethics and Professional Conduct*, https://www.aia.org/pages/3296-code-of-ethics-and-professional-conduct (accessed on November 1, 2020).

American Institute of Architects, *2018 Firm Survey Report*. Washington, DC: The American Institute of Architects, 2019. http://content.aia.org/sites/default/files/2018-08/2018-AIA-Firm-Survey-Overview.pdf (accessed on September 1, 2020).

American Medical Association, *Code of Medical Ethics*, https://www.ama-assn.org/delivering-care/ethics/code-medical-ethics-overview (accessed on September 1, 2020).

Architects Registration Board. *Architects Code: Standards of Conduct and Practice*. London: Architects Registration Board, http://www.arb.org.uk/wp-content/uploads/2016/05/Architects-Code-2017.pdf (accessed on November 1, 2020).

Anonymous, "How Midsize Engineering and Architectural Firms Prosper," *Engineering News-Record*, May 4, 2015.

Anonymous, https://www.fastcompany.com/90164300/exclusive-why-i-started-a-shitty-architecture-men-list (accessed on October 2018).

Bhabha, Homi K. "Our Neighbors, Ourselves: Contemporary Reflections on Survival," Hegel Lectures Series, https://doi.org/10.1515/9783110262445, 2011.

Benedikt, Michael. "Reality and Authenticity in the Experience Economy," *Architectural Record*, 189:11 (2001): 84–87.

Betsky, Aaron. *Queer Space: Architecture and Same Sex Desire*. New York: William Morrow, 1997.

———. "*The New York Times* Versus Architecture," *Architect*, December 23, 2014.

———. "Waiting to be Weinsteined: When Will Accusations of Sexual Harassment Arise in Architecture?" *Architect*, November 21, 2017.

Bingler, Steven, and Martin C. Peterson. "How to Rebuild Architecture," *New York Times*, December 15, 2014.

Blau, Judith R. *Architects and Firms: A Sociological Perspective on Architectural Practices*. Cambridge, MA: MIT Press, 1987.

Bloomer, Jennifer. "The Matter of the Cutting Edge," in *Desiring Practices: Architecture, Gender and the Interdisciplinary*, edited by Duncan McCorquodale, Katerina Rüedi, and Sarah Wigglesworth, 11–31. London: Black Dog, 1996.

Boettke, Peter, and Rosolino Candela. "Comparative Historical Political Economy and the Bourgeois Era," *Journal of Private Enterprise*, 32:4 (2017):13–29.
Boaz, David. "Opinion: Bourgeois Virtues," *The Guardian*, July 14, 2006.
Bourdieu, Pierre. *Distinction: A Social Critique of the Judgement of Taste*, translated by Richard Nice. Cambridge, MA: Harvard University Press, 1984.
Boyer Ernest L. and Lee D. Mitgang. *Building Community: A New Future for Architectural Education and Practice*. Princeton, NJ: Carnegie Foundation for the Advancement of Teaching, 1996.
Brown, Lori. A. *Contested Spaces: Abortion Clinics, Women's Shelters and Hospitals*. London: Taylor & Francis, 2013.
Brusset, David. "Still Allowed to Like Meier?" https://architecturehereandthere.com/2018/03/14/still-allowed-to-like-meier/ (accessed on November 1, 2020).
Bull, Malcolm. "What Is the Rational Response?" *London Review of Books* 34:10 (May 2012). Lrb.co.uk/the-paper/v34/n10/malcolmbull/what-is-the-rational-response (accessed on November 20, 2020.)
Calhoun, Craig (editor). *Habermas and the Public Sphere*. Cambridge, MA: MIT Press, 1992.
Capps, Kriston. "The 11 Worst Buildings of 2014," *Slate.com*, December 26, 2014.
Carlhian, Jean-Paul. "The Ecole des Beaux-Arts: Modes and Manners," *Journal of Architectural Education*, 33 (November 1979): 7–17.
Chase, Vanessa. "Edith Wharton, the Decoration of Houses, and Gender in Turn-of-the-Century America," in *Architecture and Feminism*, edited by Debra Coleman, Elizabeth Danze, and Carol Henderson, 130–60. New York: Princeton Architectural Press, 1996.
Chauncy, George. "Privacy Could Only Be Had in Public: Gay Uses of the Streets," in *Stud: Architectures of Masculinity*, edited by Joel Sanders, 224–68. New York: Princeton Architectural Press, 1996.
Coffay, Matthew. *The Intergenerational Ethics of Climate Change*. Bergen, Norway: University of Bergen, Department of Philosophy, 2019.
Colomina, Beatriz. "Battle Lines: E.1027," in *The Architect: Reconstructing Her Practice*, edited by Francesca Hughes, 2–25. Cambridge, MA: MIT Press, 1996.
Crawford, Margaret. "Contesting the Public Realm: Struggles Over Public Space in Los Angeles," *Journal of Architectural Education*, 49:1 (1995–96): 4–9.
Crisp, Roger, and Michael Slote (editors). *Virtue Ethics*. Oxford: Oxford University Press, 1997.
Cuff, Dana. "Collective Form: The Status of Public Architecture," *Thresholds*, 40 (2012): 55–66.
Czarnecki, John E. "Expressing the Art of Good Business," *Architectural Record*, 89:10 (October 2001): 90–108.
Dainty, Andrew (editor). *Proceedings of the 24th Annual ARCOM Conference, 1–3 September 2008*, Cardiff, UK: Association of Researchers in Construction Management, 2008.
de Graft-Johnson, A., S. Manley and C. Greed. *Why Do Women Leave Architecture?* London: RIBA, 2003. www.architecture.com/Files/RIBAProfessionalServices/Education/DiscussionPapers/WhyDoWomenLeaveArchitecture (accessed on April 2008).
de Graaf, Renier, *Four Walls and a Roof: The Complex Nature of a Simple Profession*. Cambridge, MA: Harvard University Press, 2017.
de Tocqueville, Alexis. *The Old Regime and the Revolution*, translated by John Bonner. New York: Harper & Brothers, 1856.

Dickinson, Elizabeth Evitts. "The Fifty-Year-Old Intern Architect," *Architect*, October 7, 2011. https://www.architectmagazine.com/design/the-50-year-old-intern-architect_o. (accessed on November 20, 2020).
Diderot, Denis. *Les Bijoux Indiscrets*, Project Gutenberg: https://www.gutenberg.org/files/54672/54672-h/54672-h.htm#CHAP_XXIX.(accessed on November 1, 2020).
Durning, Louise, and Mark Wrigley (editors). *Gender and Architecture*. New York: John Wiley & Sons, 2000.
Dewey, John. *Art as Experience*. New York: Capricorn Books, 1934.
Elam, Merrill. "Projects/ Recollections," in *The Architect: Reconstructing Her Practice*, edited by Francesca Hughes., 182–99. Cambridge, MA: MIT Press, 1996.
Fair Labor Standards Act, U.S. Department of Labor: https://www.dol.gov/agencies/whd/flsa (accessed on November 1, 2020).
Fanning, Bryan, and Timothy Mooney. "Pragmatism and Intolerance: Nietzsche and Rorty," *Philosophy and Social Criticism*, 36:6 (June 25, 2010): 735–55.
Faulconbridge, James R., and Daniel Muzio. "Professions in a Globalizing World: Towards a Transnational Sociology of the Professions," *International Sociology*, 26:6 (November 18, 2011): 136–52.
Fentress, Curtis. *Public Architecture: The Art Inside*. San Francisco: Oro Editions, 2011.
———. *Touchstones of Design: ReDefining Public Architecture*. Mulgrave, AU: Images Publishing, 2010.
Filler, Martin. "The Insolence of Architecture," *New York Review of Books*, June 5, 2014. Nybooks.com/articles/2014/06/05/insolence-architecture/ (accessed on November 20, 2020).
Fisher, Thomas. 'Making the Case for Higher Fees,' *Architect*, March 12, 2014. https://www.architectmagazine.com/practice/best-practices/making-the-case-for-higher-fees_o. (accessed on November 20,2020).
———. *Ethics for Architects: Fifty Dilemmas of Professional Practice*. Hudson, NY: Princeton Architectural Press, 2010.
Foucault, Michel. *Discipline and Punish*, translated by Alan Sheridan. 2nd ed. New York: Vintage Books, 1995.
Foxell, Simon. *Professionalism for the Built Environment*, London: Routledge, 2018.
Fraser, Caroline. "When Will We Care About Domestic Violence?" *New York Review of Books*, 14–16, May 28, 2020.
Fraser, Nancy. "Rethinking the Public Sphere: A Contribution to the Critique of Actually Existing Democracy," *Social Text* 25:26 (1990): 56–80.
Fustel de Coulanges, Numa Denis. *The Ancient City*. Gloucester, MA: Peter Smith, 1979 [1864].
Gardiner, Michael E. "Wild Publics and Grotesque Symposiums: Habermas and Bakhtin on Dialogue, Everyday Life and the Public Sphere," in *After Habermas: New Perspectives on the Public Sphere* edited by Nick Crossley and John Michael Roberts, 28–48. New York: Wiley–Blackwell, 2004.
Gardiner, Stephen. "A Perfect Moral Storm: Climate Change Intergenerational Ethics and the Problem of Moral Corruption," *Environmental Values*, 15:3 (2006): 397–413.
Gardiner, Stephen, Caney, S., D. Jamieson, and H. Shue (editors). *Climate Ethics: Essential Readings*. Oxford: Oxford University Press, 2010.
Gatens, Moira. *Feminism and Philosophy: Perspectives on Difference and Equality*. Bloomington, IN: Polity Press, 1991.

Gehl, Jan. *Life between Buildings: Using Public Space*, Washington, DC: Island Press, 2011.
Gehl, Jan, and Birgitte Svarre. *How to Study Public Life*. Washington, DC: Island Press, 2013.
Habermas, Jurgen. *The Structural Transformation of the Public Sphere: An Inquiry into a Category of Bourgeois Society*, Cambridge, MA: MIT Press, 1991.
Hacker, Thomas. Interview with J. M. Cava, "Our Architect: Working with Louis Kahn," *Arcade*, posted on January 26, 2016.
Hamilton, Clive. "Moral Collapse in a Warming World," *Ethics and International Affairs*, 28:3 (2014): 335–42.
Hampshire, Stuart. *Public and Private Morality*. Cambridge: Cambridge University Press, 1978.
Heathcote, Edwin. "Starchitects Risk Losing Lustre," *Financial Times*, September 8, 2011.
Held, Virginia. *Feminist Morality: Transforming Culture, Society, and Politics*. Chicago: University of Chicago Press, 1993.
Henderson, Susan R. "A Revolution in the Woman's Sphere: Grete Lihotzky and the Frankfurt Kitchen," in *Architecture and Feminism*, edited by Debra Coleman, Elizabeth Danze, and Carol Henderson,, 221–53. New York: Princeton Architectural Press, 1996.
Hochman, Elaine. *Bauhaus: Crucible of Modernism*. New York: Fromm International, 1997.
Hough, Douglas E., and Charles G. Kratz. "Can 'Good' Architecture Meet the Market Test?" *Journal of Urban Economics*, 14:1 (1983): 40–54.
Howells, John Mead. "A French Government School from the Inside," *Century Illustrated Monthly Magazine*, 62 (1901): 860–68.
———. *The École des Beaux-Arts*. New York: Architectural Record Company, 1901.
Hu, Winnie. "Hostile Architecture: How Public Spaces Keep the Public Out," *New York Times*, November 8, 2019.
———. "Times Insider: How We Searched for Hostile Architecture in New York," *New York Times*, November 8, 2019.
Huang, Te-Sheng, and Karen A. Franck. "Let's Meet at Citicorp: Can Privately Owned Public Spaces be Inclusive?" *Journal of Urban Design*, 23:4 (August 2018): 499–517.
Hughes, Will, and Cathy Hughes. "Professionalism and Professional Institutions in Times of Change," *Building Research & Information*, 41:1 (2013): 28–38.
IHS Economics: *Construction Global Outlook*, 2013. https://ihsmarkit.com/pdf/IHS_Global_Construction_ExecSummary_Feb2014_140852110913052132.pdf (accessed on February 1, 2014).
Ingraham, Catherine. "Losing It in Architecture," in *The Architect: Reconstructing Her Practice*, edited by Francesca Hughes., 148–63. Cambridge, MA: MIT Press, 1996.
Jacobs, Karrie. "Public Space in the Time of Trump," *Architect*, 3 (2017): 74–80.
Jamieson, Dale. *Reason in a Dark Time: Why the Struggle Against Climate Change Failed—and What It Means for Our Future*. New York: Oxford University Press, 2014.
Janda, Kathryn B., and Yael Parag. "A Middle-Out Approach for Improving Energy Performance in Buildings," *Building Research & Information*, 41:1 (2013): 39–50.
Kant, Immanuel 'What Is Enlightenment?' *Berlin Monthly*. 1784. Marxists.org/reference/subject/ethics/kant/enlightenment.htm (accessed on November 20, 2020).
Kaplan, Victoria. *Structural Inequality: Black Architects in the United States*. New York: Rowman and Littlefield, 2006.
Keane, Katherine. "AIA: Licensing Protects the Public," *Architect*, January 25, 2018 https://www.architectmagazine.com/practice/aia-licensing-protects-the-public_o. (accessed on November 20, 2020).
Kozlowska, Hanna. "When Buildings Are Political, Should Architects Be Politicians?" *New York Times*, September 2, 2014.

Kuttner, Robert. *Everything for Sale: The Virtues and Limits of Markets*. Chicago: University of Chicago Press, 1996.

———. "Blaming Liberalism," *New York Review of Books*, 36–38, November 21, 2019.

Larson, Magali Sarfatti. *The Rise of Professionalism: A Sociological Analysis*, Berkeley: University of California Press, 1977.

Lavin, Sylvia. "Re-Reading the Encyclopedia: Architectural Theory and the Formation of the Public in Late Eighteenth-Century France," *Journal of the Society of Architectural Historians*, 53:2 (1994): 184–92.

———. "CRITICISM: One Person at a Time," *Architectural Record*, 195:8 (August 2007): 106–17.

Lee, Stella. "Where Is Architecture's #MeToo Moment?" *New York Times*, October 12, 2018.

Macdonald, K. M. *The Sociology of the Professions*. London: Sage, 1995.

MacIntyre, Alasdair. *After Virtue: A Study in Moral Theory*. South Bend, IN: Notre Dame University Press, 1981.

MacLean, Douglas, and Peter G. Brown (editors). *Energy and the Future*. Totowa, NJ: Rowman and Littlefield, 1983.

Marx, Karl and Engels, Friedrich. *The Communist Manifesto*, https://marxists.architexturez.net/archive/marx/works/1848/communist-manifesto/ch01.htm (accessed on November 1, 2020).

Maynard, Andrew. "Work/Life/Work Balance," https://www.archdaily.com/234633/work-life-work-balance-by-andrew-maynard (accessed on September 1, 2018).

Manley, Sandra, and Ann de Graft-Johnson. "Women in Architecture: Five Years On," *Proceedings of the 24th Annual ARCOM Conference, 2008*, edited by A. Dainty. Cardiff, UK: Association of Researchers in Construction Management, 891–900.

McCloskey, Diedre N. *Bourgeois Equality: How Ideas, Not Capital or Institutions, Enriched the World*, Chicago: University of Chicago Press, 2016.

McDowell, Linda. "Spatializing Feminism," in *Bodyspace: Destabilizing Geographies of Gender and Sexuality*, ed. Nancy, Duncan., 27–46. London: Routledge, 1996.

McGuigan, Cathleen. "Architecture and the Future of the Public Realm," *Architectural Record*, 205:4 (April 1, 2017): 24.

McLeod, Mary. "Other Spaces and Others," in *The Sex of Architecture*, edited by Diana Agrest, Patricia Conway, and Leslie Kanes Weisman, 15–28.. New York: Abrams Publishers, 1996.

Morrell, Paul. "Collaboration for Change: The Edge Commission Report on the Future of Professionalism," https://edgedebate.com/blog/collaboration-for-change-amp-the-core-cities (accessed on November 1, 2020).

Morris, Meaghan. "Great Moments in Social Climbing: King Kong and the Human Fly," in *Sexuality and Space*, edited by Beatriz Colomina., 1–52. New York: Princeton Architectural Press, 1992.

Morrison, Mary L. (editor). *Historic Savannah: Survey of Significant Buildings in the Historic and Victorian Districts of Savannah, Georgia*, Savannah: Historic Savannah Foundation and The Junior League of Savannah, 1979.

Murdoch, Iris. 'The Sovereignty of Good over other Concepts,' in *Virtue Ethics*, edited by Roger Crisp and Michael Slote., 99–117. Oxford: Oxford University Press, 1997.

National Organization of Minority Architects. *NOMA Magazine*. Fall, 2020.

National Society of Professional Engineers. *2003 Code of Ethics*. Alexandria, VA: National Society of Professional Engineers, 2003.

Németh, Jeremy. "Defining a Public: The Management of Privately Owned Public Space," *Urban Studies*, 46:11 (2009): 2463–90.
Németh, Jeremy, and Stephen Schmidt. "The Privatization of Public Space: Modeling and Measuring Publicness," *Environment and Planning B: Planning and Design*, 38 (2011): 5–23.
Newitz, Annalee. "A Better Social Media World Is Waiting for Us," *New York Times*, November 30, 2019.
Nietzsche, Frederich. *Uber die Zunkunft unserer Bildungsantalten* in *Werke III* (Munich: Carl Hanser, 1966), 189. as quoted in Bourdieu, Pierre. *Distinction: A Social Critique of the Judgement of Taste*. Cambridge, MA: Harvard University Press, 1984.
Ockman, Joan. "The YES Man," *Architecture*, 91:3 (2002): 76–79.
Olcayto, Rory. "Take an Ethical Stance, Libeskind Tells his Peers," *Building Design*, 3. February 15, 2008.
Oud, J. J. P. "Art and Machine," *De Stijl*, 1:3 (1918) 25–27.
Pauker, Benjamin, "Frank Gehry." *Foreign Policy*, 201 (July/August, 2013): 24.
Pawley, Martin. *The Private Future: Causes and Consequences of Community Collapse in the West*. London: Thames and Hudson, 1973.
Pearson, Clifford A. "Making Good Design Pay Off," *Architectural Record*, (October, 2000): 84–106.
Piketty, Thomas. *Capital in the Twenty-First Century*, translated by Arthur Goldhammer. Cambridge, MA: Belknap Press, 2014.
Pine, Joseph B., and James H. Gilmore. *The Experience Economy*. Cambridge, MA: Harvard Business Press, 1999.
Punday, Daniel. "Foucault's Body Tropes," *New Literary History*, 31 (2000): 509–28.
Putnam, Robert. *Bowling Alone: The Collapse and Revival of American Community*. New York: Simon and Schuster, 2000.
Ray, Nicholas. "Bibliotecas nacionales en la ciudad europea del siglo veinte: Londres y Paris," in *Biblioteca, Ciudad y Sociedad: Plan Maestro Biblioteca Nacional de Chile*, 74–91. Santiago: Biblioteca Nacional de Chile.
Rendell, Jane. "Only Resist: A Feminist Approach to Critical Spatial Practice," *The Architectural Review*, February 19, 2018. https://www.architectural-review.com/essays/only-resist-a-feminist-approach-to-critical-spatial-practice (accessed on November 20, 2020).
Riach, James. "Zaha Hadid Defends World Cup Role Following Migrant Worker Deaths," *The Guardian*, February 25, 2014.
Richter, Dagmar, "A Practice of One's Own: The Critical Copy and Translation of Space," in *The Architect: Reconstructing Her Practice*, edited by Francesca Hughes, 96–127. Cambridge, MA: MIT Press, 1996.
Rorty, Richard. *Objectivity, Relativism and Truth: Philosophical Papers*, volume 1. Cambridge: Cambridge University Press, 1990.
———. *Truth and Progress: Philosophical Papers*, volume 3. Cambridge: Cambridge University Press, 1993.
———. "What's Wrong with 'Rights,'" 15–18, *Harper's Magazine*, June 1996. Also at: https://www.thefreelibrary.com/What%27s+wrong+with+%22rights.%22(excerpt+from+a+speech+by+Richard...-a018311735. (accessed on November 20, 2020).
Royal Institute of British Architects. *Code of Professional Conduct*, London: RIBA. https://www.architecture.com/knowledge-and-resources/resources-landing-page/code-of-professional-conduct#:~:text=Honesty%2C%20integrity%20and%20competence%2C%20as,effect%20on%201%20May%202019 (accessed on May 1, 2019).

Russell, James S. "Good Design is Good Business: Second Annual Business Week/ Architectural Record Awards," *Architectural Record*, 186.10 (October, 1998): 88–102.

———. "Taking the Measure of Design and the Bottom Line," *Architectural Record*, 187.10 (October, 1999): 84–104.

Sandel, Michael J. *Democracy's Discontent: America In Search of a Public Philosophy*, Cambridge MA: Harvard University Press, 1996.

Scheffler, Samuel. *The Afterlife*, The Tanner Lectures on Human Values, Berkeley: University of California, March 13–15, 2012.

Schmidt, Stephen, Jeremy Nemeth, and Erik Botsford. "The Evolution of Privately Owned Public Spaces in New York City," *Urban Design International*, 16:4 (Winter 2011): 270–84.

Scott Brown, Denise. "Room at the Top? Sexism and the Star System in Architecture," in *Architecture: A Place for Women*, edited by Ellen Berkeley, 237–46. Washington: Smithsonian Institution Press, 1989.

———. "Through the Looking Glass," in *The Sex of Architecture*, edited by Diana Agrest, Patricia Conway, and Leslie Kanes Weisman., 211–16. New York: Abrams Publishers, 1996.

Sen, Amartya. *Development as Freedom*. New York: Anchor Books, 1999.

———. "The Global Reach of Human Rights," *Journal of Applied Philosophy*, 29:2 (2012): 91–100.

Shubow, Justin. "Architecture Continues to Implode: More Insiders Admit the Profession Is Failing," *Forbes*, January 6, 15.

Stein, Karen D. "Good Design Is Good Business," *Architectural Record*, 185:10 (October, 19/97): 54–64.

Stevens, Garry. *The Favored Circle*. Cambridge, MA: MIT Press, 1998.

Stewart, Evan, and Douglas Hartmann. "The New Structural Transformation of the Public Sphere," in *Sociological Theory*, 38:2 (June 4, 2020): 170–91.

Stratigakos, Despina. *Where Are the Women Architects?* Princeton: Princeton University Press, 2016.

Sutherland, Stewart. "Scottish Enlightenment," https://www.britannica.com/event/Scottish-Enlightenment also in *Encyclopaedia Britannica: The Ideas That Made the Modern World* (Britannica Guides Series) *The People, Philosophy and History of the Enlightenment*, 2008 (accessed on November 1, 2020).

Sutton, Sharon. "Resisting the Patriarchal Norms of Professional Education,' in *The Sex of Architecture*, edited by Diana Agrest, Patricia Conway, and Leslie Kanes Weisman, 287–94. New York: Abrams Publishers, 1996.

Tanzer, Kim, and Caroline Constant. "Center for Women's Studies and Gender Research, University of Florida, 1994–2000," *Journal of Architectural Education*, 55:2 (November 2001): 81–89.

Tauber, Susanne, Martijn van Zomeren, and Maja Kutlaca. "Should the Moral Core of Climate Issues be Emphasized or Downplayed in Public Discourse?" *Climatic Change*, 130:3 (2015): 453–64.

Taylor, Charles, *Philosophical Arguments*. Cambridge, MA: Harvard University Press, 1995.

Taylor, Scott. "Book Review," *Organizational Studies*, 38:I (2017): 151–53.

Thatcher, Margaret. interviewed in *Woman's Own*, 9/23/1987, full interview online at: https://www.margaretthatcher.org/document/106689 (accessed on November 1, 2020).

Till, Jeremy. *Architecture Depends*. Cambridge MA: MIT Press, 2013.

Tronto, Joan. *Moral Boundaries: A Political Argument for an Ethic of Care*. New York: Routledge, 1994.

Vale, Brenda. "Gender and an Architecture of Environmental Responsibility," in *Desiring Practices: Architecture, Gender and the Interdisciplinary*, edited by Duncan McCorquodale, Katerina Rüedi, and Sarah Wigglesworth, London: Black Dog, 1996.

Vandell, Kerry D., and Jonathan S. Lane. "The Economics of Architecture and Urban Design: Some Preliminary Findings," *AREUA: Journal of the American Real Estate & Urban Economics Association*, 17:2 (Summer 1989): 235–60.

———. "Economics of Office Design," *ULI Research Working Paper Series*, paper 603. Washington, DC: Urban Land Institute, July 1992.

Villa, Dana. "Postmodernism and the Public Sphere," *American Political Science Review*, 86:3 (1992): 712–21.

Wainwright, Oliver. "Architecture Furlough Fraud, Snooping and Firings: Architects Speak Out over Lockdown Exploitation," *The Guardian*, October 12, 2020.

Walker, Margaret Urban. "Moral Understandings: Alternative 'Epistemology' for a Feminist Ethics," in *Explorations in Feminist Ethics*, edited by Eve Browning Cole and Susan Coultrap-McQuin, 165–75. Bloomington: University of Indiana Press, 1992.

Ward, Jacob. "Won't You Be My Neighbor?" in *Architecture*, 91:4 (April, 2002): 72.

Warner, Michael. *Publics and Counterpublics*. New York: Zone Books, 2005.

Watkin, David. *George III and the Culture of the Enlightenment*. London: Royal Collection Publications, 2004, Frontispiece.

Weisman, Leslie Kanes. *Discrimination by Design*. Urbana: University of Illinois Press, 1992.

White, Stephen K. (editor). *The Cambridge Companion to Habermas*. Cambridge: Cambridge University Press, 1995.

Whitechurch, Celia. "Shifting Identities and Blurring Boundaries: The Emergence of *Third Space* Professionals in UK Higher Education," *Higher Education Quarterly*, 62:4 (2008): 377–96.

Whiting, Sarah. "Architecture and Dispersal," *Architectural Design*, edited by Rafi Segal and Els Verbakel, 78:1 (January/February 2008): 102–7.

Williamson, Roxanne Kuter. *American Architects and the Mechanics of Fame*. Austin: University of Texas Press, 1991.

Zimmerman, Michael. "Globalization, Multiculturalism, and Architectural Ethics," in *Architecture, Ethics and Globalization*, edited by Graham Owen, 158–70. New York: Routledge, 2009.

INDEX

Abdel-Nour, Farid 47, 50
Allen, Stan 109
American College of Healthcare
    Architects (ACHA) 132
American Institute of Architects (AIA)
    11, 26
  AIA Code of Ethics 19, 21
  amendments to Code of Ethics 93, 94
  buildings as infrastructure 110
American Medical Association 17
America's Castles 66
ARB Standards of Conduct and
    Practice 16, 21
Architectural Record 8, 18, 27, 37

Baier, Annette 85
Bell, Clive 97
Benedikt, Michael 68, 113, 119
Bentham, Jeremy utilitarianism 60, 68
Betsky, Aaron 14
  *Queer Space: Architecture and Same Sex
    Desire* 91, 95
Bibliothèque Nationale 125
Bingler, Steven and Peterson,
    Martin C. 14
Black Lives Matter 78
Black Visions 78
Blau, Judith R. 31
Blondel, Jacques François *Architecture
    Francoise* 60
Bloomer, Jennifer "The Matter of the
    Cutting Edge" 104
Boettke, Peter and Candela,
    Rosolino 57, 58
Boulée, Étienne-Louis 60
Bourdieu, Pierre 15
Boyer, Ernest L. and Mitgang, Lee D. 9

Bricktown, Oklahoma City 120
British National Library 124
Brown, Lori A. 104
buildings as infrastructure 108–10
Bull, Malcolm 136
Bureau of Labor Statistics 42, 94
Bauhaus 5
Bottom Line Public Spaces (BLPS) 108
Business Week 28

Carlhian, Jean-Paul 5
Carnegie Foundation Report 9, 10
Capitol Mall 114–15
Carroll, Noël moderate moralism 97
Chambers, William 3
Chauncey, George 91
Coffay, Matthew 134
Colomina, Beatriz 87
Congressional Budget Office
    report 41
Consequentialism 88
Crawford, Margaret 108–9
Cuff, Dana 109

De Graaf, Renier 3
De Tocqueville, Alexis 59
Dewey, John 117–18
Diderot, Denis *Les Bijoux Indiscrets* 57
Diderot, Denis and d'Alembert,
    Jean le Rond 59
Durand, J. N. L. 60

Ecole des Beaux-Arts 4, 5
*Edge Commission Report on the Future of
    Professionalism* 18
Egyptian pyramids 101
Eisenman, Peter 70

Fair Labor Standards 10
Fentress, Curtis *Public Architecture,
   Touchstones of Design: Redefining Public
   Architecture* 55
Filler, Martin 45
Fisher, Thomas 4, 45
Foucault, Michel 140
Foxell, Simon 16
Faulconbridge, James R. and Muzio,
   Daniel 45
Franklin, Benjamin 58
Fraser, Nancy 81, 83, 90, 93
Fustel de Coulanges, Numa Denis 55

Gardiner, Michael E. 62
Gardiner, Stephen 134
Gaut, Berys moralism 97
Gehl, Jan *How to Study Public Life, Life
   Between Buildings: How to Study Public
   Space* 55
Gehry, Frank 3
Gender pay equity 94
Gilligan, Carol, *In a Different Voice* 85
Good Design is Good Business
   awards 27–29
Greek Revival 98
Gropius, Walter 5

Habermas Jürgen 58, 61–65, 137, 140
Hadid, Zaha 45, 50, 94
Halsband, Frances 93
Hamilton, Clive 134
Hamlet 97, 100
Hampshire, Stuart 67
Heathcote, Edwin 50
Held, Virginia 84
Historic Savannah Foundation 105
Hough, Douglas and Kratz, Charles
   30–31, 36
Hostile architecture 111
Howells, John Mead 5, 6
Huang, Te-Sheng and Franck,
   Karen A. 113
Hughes, Will and Cathy 136
Hunter, Anna Colquitt 105–6

Income inequality 40–42
   in architecture 43–44
Isaiah Davenport House, Savannah 105

Jacobson, Daniel 97
Jamieson, Dale 134
Jefferson, Thomas 7
John, Eileen opportunistic moralism 97
Justice reasoning 85

Kahn, Louis 6
Kant, Immanuel categorical imperative 51
   on Enlightenment 57
Koolhaas, Rem 45
Kuttner, Robert 66, 137

LGBT Community Center, San
   Francisco 91
Large Firm Roundtable (LFRT) 80
Lavin, Sylvia 121, 123
Ledoux, Claude Nicolas 60
Lee, Stella 6, 8
Libeskind, Daniel 45
Lin Maya Vietnam Veterans Memorial 70
Loos, Adolph 69, 77

MacDonald, K. M. 57, 60
MacIntyre, Alisdair 72–77
Marx, Karl 61
Marshall, Michael 80
Maynard, Andrew 7
Mayne, Thom 109
McCloskey, Diedre 22, 56–57
McGuigan, Cathleen 110
Meier, Richard 95
Memorial to the Murdered Jews of
   Europe 70
Middle-out approach 136
Mondrian, Piet 28
Morell, Paul 18

National Fire Protection Association
   (NFPA) 131
National Council of Architectural
   Registration Boards (NCARB) 131
National Organization of Minority
   Architects (NOMA) 78–79
National September 11 Memorial &
   Museum (9/11 Memorial) 71
National Society of Professional
   Engineers 17
Németh, Jeremy and Schmidt,
   Stephen 111–12

INDEX

Neoliberal economics 65
Newitz, Annalee 139
Noddings, Nel 85

Occupy Wall Street 62
Oculus, New York 125
Oklahoma City National Memorial 70–71
Oud, J. J. P. 124
Owen, Graham *Architecture Ethics and Globalization* 45

Paglia, Camille 104
Parfit, Derek identity problem 134
Pawley, Martin 67
Piketty, Thomas *Capital in the Twenty-First Century* 39–40
Pine, Joseph and Gilmore, James 67
Polis 13, 59
Privately Owned Public Spaces (POPS) 111–13
Procedural (liberal) democracy 65
Project Pipeline 79
Public choice theory 65
Putnam, Robert *Bowling Alone: The Collapse and Revival of American Community* 66

Quatramère de Quincy 123

Racist architecture in the South 96–102
RIBA 9
RIBA Code of Professional Conduct 16, 21, 60
Rorty, Richard 47–51
Rowe's Wharf, Boston 115

San Francisco Federal Building 121, 123
San Francisco City Hall 124
San Francisco Academy of Sciences 124
Sandel, Michael 117
Scheffler, Samuel 133–34
Scott Brown, Denise 4, 6
Sen, Amartya 51

Sennett, Richard, *The Fall of Public Man* 66
"Shitty Architecture Men" 93
Smith, Adam 58
Soane, Sir John 60
Soft infrastructure 110
Stevens, Garry, *The Favored Circle* 8
Stewart, Evan and Hartmann, Douglas 137
Sutherland, Stewart 58

Tahrir Square 62
Tanzer, Kim and Constant, Caroline, Center for Women's Studies and Gender Research 92
Tauber, Susanne, van Zomeren, Martijn and Kutlaca, Maja 135
Taylor, Charles 59–60
Taylor, Scott 58
Thatcher, Margaret 65
"The 50–Year-old Intern Architect," 44
third space 104
Till, Jeremy 17
Tronto, Joan 85–86, 88

UK study of women in the architecture profession 94
U.S. District Courts, Salt Lake City 123
utilitarianism 67

Vale, Brenda 88
Vandell, Kerry 30–36
Villa, Dana 108

Walker, Margaret Urban 85
Ward, Jacob 91
Warner, Michael counterpublics 77
Whiting, Sarah 107–8
Williamson, Roxanne 7, 8

Zimmerman, Michael "Globalization, Multiculturalism and Architectural Ethics" 45

www.ingramcontent.com/pod-product-compliance
Lightning Source LLC
Chambersburg PA
CBHW021143230426
43667CB00005B/233